Letters
from the
Father's
Heart

by Ann Yeager

Unless otherwise noted, Scripture quotations are from The Holy Bible, New International Version® (NIV®), Copyright ©1973, 1978, 1984 by International Bible Society. Used by permission of Zondervan. All rights reserved.

Printed in the United States of America

ISBN: 978-0-9982937-0-7

Acknowledgements

I want to thank my husband, Chuck, my son, Justin, and daughter, Laura, for their encouragement and guidance; I also want to thank my daughter, Laura, for the cover photograph; Pastor Dan Allen for his guidance in publishing; Ann Small, Suzan Mann, and Denise Weiss, for proofreading and editing; and my pastor, Walter Carter, for pastoring and encouraging the prophetic gift. Finally, I want to thank my Heavenly Father—my Daddy—for sharing His heart with me and providing the way to share it with others.

I would love to hear your comments
or how this book has changed your life.
Reach me at annyeager.com or
www.facebook.com/lettersfromthefathersheart.

Ann Yeager

Endorsements

"I would like to recommend going on a journey with Ann Yeager in her book, *Letters from the Father's Heart.* Her brief devotional interactions with God act as an invitation for readers to hear from God for themselves. This devotional book will enrich your life and help you to dive deeper into the heart of your loving Heavenly Father."

—Benjamin Williams, Author of Basics in 21 Days, Founder of Life Ministries International, Pastor of Convergence Center, Administrator of Global School of Supernatural Ministry, GSI, OnlineSatellite

"Letters from the Father's Heart, by Ann Yeager, contains healing prayers and wonderful counsel from God to each of us. The really nice thing is, we can all hear God's voice, every day, as we walk with Him in the cool of the day. Although this is simple, it took me years to discover that the voice of the Holy Spirit within me is experienced as flowing thoughts which light upon my mind as my eyes are fixed on Jesus (Jn. 7:37-39; Heb. 12:1-2). The awesome gift of the New Covenant is that the Holy Spirit now lives within our hearts. Each of us can hear and write down His flow of thoughts, just as Ann has done. King David did it as he wrote the Psalms. The Apostle John did it as he wrote the book of Revelation. Many others in the Bible did it also. Many are doing it today. You can too. It is not hard! Thank you Ann for demonstrating that the Bible can be lived and blessing us with this Wonderful Counsel from Almighty God."

—Dr. Mark Virkler, President of Communion With God Ministries

"Just keeping up with the daily pressures of life and the pace that it requires can yield a heart full of worry and anxiety with little to show for it. It is too easy to allow these daily stresses to distract us from the one thing that can help us. That one thing is to encounter the Fathers heart. *Letters from the Fathers Heart* will draw you away from the hurriedness of the day and all it's pull. You will not only hear what our loving Heavenly Father is tenderly speaking but you will begin to feel the rest and refreshing deep in your soul that comes from being with Him and hearing his voice speak to your most inner being. I recommend that you journey with Ann each day into a deeper and more intimate place of rest with The Father."

—Shane Lilly, Pastor of Ministries. Church on the Hill, Fishersville, VA

"Ann is a dear friend who believes in worshiping Jesus in spirit and in truth. With some people it's 50% of each—not with Ann. With her; it's 100% spirit, 100% truth. This devotional book will build you up, encourage you, and release hope over your life in the spirit of kindness and celebration. She is a person of character and integrity with an absolute passion for the presence of God in a tangible way. I pray that you read this daily word with an open heart and contemplate your personal activation based in the content of this devotional."

—Jim Heidrick, Lead Pastor Firewheel Church San Diego, CA

"Ann Yeager is a great friend. As her pastor we shared many times where we prayed with and for one another. It is so fitting that this Devotional would be called, *Letters from the Father's Heart,* because all the years I knew her, that is exactly what she did: she sought God's heart. At times the Lord would prompt her to share what she had been hearing with others. Always it was an encouraging word, but more than that it was also a word that had the power of God within it therefore the word was indeed life and light. At one of the lowest and darkest points in my pastoral ministry Ann, her husband Chuck, and two other good friends Bob and Barb Foster came knocking on my door, and it was like an incarnation of God's presence. Her words, along with the prayers of these 'people of God' turned me around that evening. They set me back on the path of confidence in who I was before the LORD with a reassurance of my calling as the leader of the congregation God had privileged me to serve. Best of all, peace again reigned in my heart. My prayer for you who read these words is for you to be impacted the same way I was. Ann is the instrument God is using, but it is God speaking from His own heart to yours. May you too receive God's Grace and Peace."

—James Carver, Pastor of Sanctuary United Methodist Church North Wales, PA

"My endorsement of *Letters from the Father's Heart* is not as much an endorsement of the book as it is the endorsement of its author, Ann Yeager. In the ten years I've known her, I have watched and witnessed her passion and gifting to see and to hear Father's heart grow and grow. A passion and gifting to see Him, His face, and what He is doing and to hear His voice and His heart. Two delights I've experienced along the way in times, now, too numerous to count. First, the encouragement of the words—both spontaneously and through these letters— she has shared with me personally and with our church in worship. Second, and most delightfully, their timeliness. Either she has me under surveillance, or she is tuned in to the Holy Spirit who oversees my hearing, preparation and need. What can be overlooked and even lost in writing words down is Ann's heart and humility. Her heart aches and breaks for Father's children. I've seen this over and over again through her tears. Her humility shines with the childlike wonder with which she submits the words. I have never known her to promote herself. Ann is one of God's treasures to our congregation, and one of His treasures to me. May this book become a treasure for you. To endorse the reading of *Letters from the Father's Heart* is not enough. I encourage you to take your time to read and digest the small portions submitted here portion by portion; read slowly, read out loud, and re-read. Allow Father to minister the fullness of His heart to you."

—Walter S. Carter, Lead Pastor, First UMC, Ephrata, PA

Introduction

I have been seeking "more" of the Lord for twenty years. I wasn't content just to go to church and pray, but then to go about my daily life without Him. When our pastor at the time, Jim Carver, said that God "isn't about a religion but about a relationship," a light bulb went off. I started to pursue Him by asking to have His heart so that I could begin to love like He does and to have His mind so that I could begin to think like He does and understand His ways. I wanted to see what He sees and do what He does. Countless hours have been spent in His presence pursuing Him. My life is so much fuller, richer, and more peaceful as a result.

It wasn't always that way, though. In my early adult years, I struggled with wanting to be the perfect wife, mother, and person. I suffered from severe anxiety attacks but told no one, not even my husband, because I thought Christians shouldn't have problems. I was so wrong!

In June of 2014, in my pursuit of "more," I attended the Global Awakening Summer Intensive School (GSI)— Randy Clark's school in Mechanicsburg, PA—where I spent three weeks with other people from around the world, hungry and thirsty for more, and it was life changing for me. I have read many of the publications of Global Awakening and Bethel Church in CA. But I have learned the most by reading God's word, which I believe is infallible, and by listening to Him teach me over the years out of the intimate relationship we have. Somewhere along this journey, I realized I was hearing from Him in new ways. I knew that the words coming into my mind were not my own! As I continued this new journey and hungered for more, I began getting messages for other people—words from Him—that were encouraging and loving. I realized He was giving me my heart's desire: to know His heart!

In October of 2014, He gave me a message for the people at the church I attend. It was very similar to the letters in this book. I shared it with my pastor, Walter Carter, and he said he wanted me to share it with our congregation, that it was "Father's heart." That week, while I was out mowing the grass, I was reflecting on the words—how encouraging they were, how His sharing His heart for us provided so much hope; I was also thinking about Walter's words—that it was Father's heart. Suddenly I heard the Lord say, "Ann, I want you to write a book." I stopped in my tracks, and after a moment of being stunned, I replied, "I can't write. I don't like to write and I have nothing to say." He immediately countered, "But I do know how to write and I do have something to say." He then went on to share with me that He wanted me to write a 365 day devotional book and He even gave me the title, *Letters from the Father's Heart*. He said it would be written in first person as if He were speaking directly to us. He wanted to share His heart with all of us. I became so emotional as I sensed His great love for us and His desire to share that love and to have us know His heart. Then I came back to reality and thought: "I don't even know how I could write 30 letters let alone 365!" I said to Him, "This is going to have to be from you Lord, because I can't do it on my own." Even though I doubted my ability, I didn't doubt the God I have grown to know so well.

As I finished mowing, I thought about the teachings of Dr. Mark Virkler, one of my instructors at GSI, who suggested just to stay connected to Him and let the writing flow. I recalled how he called me a prophet and gave me the encouragement that others see the gift the Lord has given me. I went to my computer, brought up a blank page and said, "Lord, if this is from you, show me what to say." The words just came, and have continued to come over the year and a half this project has taken!

What is so amazing is that there have been many times when I have read the letter that I heard Him say, and it was just what I needed to hear! That is so like Him! Even more amazing is that He wrote letters that equipped me to handle issues that eventually arose in my life when my husband's and my life were changed in an instant. We experienced firsthand the ugliness of sin in mankind, but also the goodness of God! Even though our lives have been radically changed, and still at times are very difficult, I reread, and more importantly, applied to my life, those letters dealing with forgiveness and how to go on through the storms of life with peace, hope, and joy!

My prayer is that you read these letters searching for Father's Heart in each one. Some of these letters may jump out at you as they did for me. Some letters may not be what you need at the moment, but might be what someone else needs that you can share with them. Some you may recall later in life when you face a situation He addresses in His letter.

I sense that our Father wants us to read each letter and ponder it. I sense He wants us to then ask Him the question, "What are you saying specifically to me from this letter?" Write down what He says. I believe He desires interaction with us and wants to know what you are saying to Him in response. Write that down, too.

I sense that He wants us not just to read these letters and think "that was really good advice," but to use His words to us to change the way we think and act and to bring us to a place where we live out of His power and love. Father's heart wants us to experience His peace and joy no matter what we are facing in our lives. His greatest desire is to have a close and personal relationship with us. Read now His letters to us, and come to know Father's heart!

—Ann Yeager

JANUARY 1

I know you struggle sometimes with relating to Me as your Heavenly Father. You may not have had an earthly father in your life, or he may have been distant or unloving. You can't seem to get past your view of your dad to relate to Me as your Heavenly Father. My child, those are lies that you are believing that I am just like your dad. Satan is doing everything he can to prevent you from coming to Me. Holding on to this wrong thinking can make it difficult for you to have a relationship with Me. Clear your mind of all thoughts of this nature. Start afresh getting to know Me through My Word, by just spending time with Me, and even through these letters which reveal My heart to you. Your earthly father, even if he was kind, wasn't perfect and therefore was incapable of loving you with a perfect love. But My love for you is perfect. As you get to know Me, you will come to know how I am guiding, protecting and providing for you. My child, please give Me a chance and let Me into your life.

But God demonstrates his own love for us in this: While we were still sinners, Christ died for us.
—Romans 5:8

See what great love the Father has lavished on us, that we should be called children of God!
And that is what we are! The reason the world does not know us is that it did not know him.
—1 John 3:1

JANUARY 2

I am always with you. Never for a moment will I leave you. Even if you take a break from Me, or when you mess-up or when you don't put Me first, I am still there by your side. I won't ever give up on you. I am the one constant in your life that you can count on. I am an active part in your daily life, and I go everywhere with you. I would love for you to become aware of My continual presence and how that can change you. It is when you are going through a trial that I am the closest to you. I am there when you wake up at night worried and panicked. You can trust and depend on Me. I would love for you to talk to Me more and involve Me in everything about your life. Please tell Me what it is that bothers you, what you fear, what you enjoy, or what makes you laugh. I created you for a relationship with Me, and I love you so much!

Be strong and courageous. Do not be afraid or terrified because of them, for the Lord your God
goes with you; he will never leave you nor forsake you. The Lord himself goes before you and will
be with you; he will never leave you nor forsake you. Do not be afraid; do not be discouraged.
—Deuteronomy 31:6, 8

JANUARY 3

$\mathcal{T}$his is the start of a new year, and there are lots of choices and decisions to make. Will you live your life for Me or for yourself? Will you make Me your first priority or follow the ways of the world? Will you settle for instant gratification or eternal rewards? Ask Me for help. I can take away your desire for what is not pleasing to Me. I can give you a heart for what is in My heart. Come, learn from the one who loves you unconditionally. The path you choose to take is up to you. Choose wisely, My dear one; I so desire for you to be at peace.

But the Helper, the Holy Spirit, whom the Father will send in My name, He will teach you all things, and bring to your remembrance all that I said to you.
—John 14:26 (NASB)

Therefore anyone who sets aside one of the least of these commands and teaches others accordingly will be called least in the kingdom of heaven, but whoever practices and teaches these commands will be called great in the kingdom of heaven.
—Matthew 5:19

JANUARY 4

$\mathcal{W}$hen you find yourself feeling stressed, and your mind is going a million directions at once and you can't seem to find Me, please take a moment and just breathe! Take a deep breath and breathe in My presence. Do that a few times, especially in highly stressful times. As you are doing this, consciously let go of all the thoughts in your mind battling for your attention. Let them go, and start to relax your body. Quiet your mind and heart and intentionally be still before Me. It is then you will find Me and connect to Me, and I can help you.

Be still before the Lord and wait patiently for him; do not fret when people succeed in their ways, when they carry out their wicked schemes.
—Psalm 37:7

He says, "Be still, and know that I am God; I will be exalted among the nations, I will be exalted in the earth."
—Psalm 46:10

JANUARY 5

*M*y child, I want you to become aware of what you are thinking. If any of your thoughts cause you pain or any kind of negative emotion, these thoughts are not from Me. I want you to consciously recognize them and immediately stop thinking about them. This may take some practice, and you may have to do it quite often, but it is worth the effort. I want very much for you to feel My peace. This is so different from what you feel when you are thinking about the lies. After you stop focusing on the negative thoughts, I want you to consciously fill your mind with who I am to you! I am your rock, encourager, comforter, protector, peace, strength, guide, healer, deliverer, and provider. Meditate on Me and who I am to you for every situation you face, and feel My peace start to flow over you.

We demolish arguments and every pretension that sets itself up against the knowledge of God, and we take captive every thought to make it obedient to Christ.
—2 Corinthians 10:5

See to it that no one takes you captive through hollow and deceptive philosophy, which depends on human tradition and the elemental spiritual forces of this world rather than on Christ.
—Colossians 2:8

JANUARY 6

*T*he enemy lurks around and is continually ready to pounce at the opportune time. He knows how to lure you in. He constantly reminds you of all your mistakes, weaknesses and sins. He sets you up to live an endless cycle of comparison and competition with other people. He makes you feel ashamed, guilty and unworthy. I share what he can do to you so you become aware of when he is trying to wreak havoc on your life. But the good news is that he is a defeated foe! Do not dwell on him—ever. Dwell on My promise that "greater is He that is in you, than he that is in the world!" Choose not to believe his lies. I chose you to be holy and blameless in Me. I predestined you as My adopted child. I have redeemed you and have forgiven you because of My son's work on the cross. These are truths to dwell on!

You, dear children, are from God and have overcome them, because the one who is in you is greater than the one who is in the world.
—1 John 4:4

For he chose us in him before the creation of the world to be holy and blameless in his sight. In love he predestined us for adoption to sonship through Jesus Christ, in accordance with his pleasure and will.
—Ephesians 1:4-5

JANUARY 7

*H*ow many times do you catch yourself saying or thinking, "what if" about a certain situation? You fret about what may happen, and your mind wanders to a number of scenarios about how something could turn out. I want you to know there are no "what-if's"! That thought is not from Me. I want you to rest in My peace. No matter what happens in your life, I am right there with you being Lord of every situation. I give you what you need at the very time you need it. When you need guidance, I show you the way. If it's comfort, strength or peace you seek, I pour into you all that you need. I provide, heal, and protect. I walk with you every step of the way and sometimes carry you when you can't go any further. Remember, there are no "what-if's". Look to Me instead!

Let the peace of Christ rule in your hearts, since as members of one body you were called to peace. And be thankful.
—Colossians 3:15

If we are thrown into the blazing furnace, the God we serve is able to deliver us from it, and he will deliver us from Your Majesty's hand. But even if he does not, we want you to know, Your Majesty, that we will not serve your gods or worship the image of gold you have set up.
—Daniel 3:17-18

JANUARY 8

*T*here are bandaids all over your body. They cover over all the things in your life you have not yet turned over to Me and, for whatever reason, want to hold on to. These bandaids cover and hide unforgiveness, shame, worry, anger, rejection, regrets, unworthiness, pride, and all the things that are not from Me that bring you distress. On the outside you seem fine, but on the inside, it is eating away at you. My Son died for this very reason. I loved you that much! Jesus' blood washes over all of these things and wipes them away forever. It grieves My heart to see you suffer. Allow Me to gently peel away the bandaids and set you free. There may be some discomfort, and it is a process, but I am right there by your side, cheering you on to freedom and peace! Open your mind and heart to Me and who I am to you.

Being confident of this, that he who began a good work in you will carry it on to completion until the day of Christ Jesus.
—Philippians 1:6

JANUARY 9

*T*rust with your heart, even though you don't see anything happening. Even though you don't hear Me or feel anything, I am there ministering to you when you aren't even aware. I am there to guide and direct you and to lovingly keep you on the right pathway. I am there to protect you as I shield you from harm. I give you support and undergird you. I am the one constant in your life that will not change—ever. My promises are true yesterday, today and always! Nothing will keep Me from loving you with all that I am. I am right by your side and will never leave you. Please believe My promises and reach out for Me. Nothing is more important to Me than your well-being.

Jesus Christ is the same yesterday and today and forever.

—Hebrews 13:8

Blessed is the one who trusts in the Lord, who does not look to the proud, to those who turn aside to false gods.

—Psalm 40:4

JANUARY 10

*D*o you know how much I love you? You are My prized possession! I created you and you are My masterpiece! I did not make a mistake. Your parents weren't a mistake either. All of this is to reveal My glory. Nothing about you is a mistake. Everything you have gone through and have experienced can be used for good. Your past does not define you. It does not have to have any lasting effect on your life. You are delivered, healed and made whole. Make it yours, for this is a new day and you are a new creation! I am your loving Father, and I want the best for you. I am by your side guiding you. Choose this new life, and turn away from the pain of your former life.

And we know that in all things God works for the good of those who love him who have been called according to his purpose.

—Romans 8:28

Therefore, if anyone is in Christ, the new creation has come: The old has gone, the new is here!
—2 Corinthians 5:17

You grew up going to church and Sunday school and came from a Christian family. But when you left home, you stopped going. You think about Me from time to time and even pray, but the busyness of life and other priorities have gotten in the way. You haven't really rejected Me, but you don't really see a need for Me, and you want to do things on your own. You might have even been hurt by church people or a pastor and see Me in the same light; but My nature is to never hurt you. It's important to Me that you know I have never stopped loving you or wanting you to come back to Me. I will never give up on you! There is so much I can help you with to make your life easier if you would allow Me in. Growing up, you only got to know of Me, which is not the same as getting to know Me in a personal relationship. You had a religion, not a relationship, and there is a huge difference! Get to know the real Me by talking with people who have an established relationship with Me, reading My Word, and just spending time with Me. Tell Me your frustrations, concerns, and what you are passionate about. Be a part of a Bible-believing church family and establish friendships with others already walking with Me. What I can give you besides eternal life, which you already know about, is abundant life for now! Abundant life is living a life connected to My strength, guidance, provision, and peace, no matter what crisis or situation you face! You do not have to be stressed out or let worries consume you. Learn about these and other promises I make to you in the Bible. I love you My child. My Son died on the cross thinking of you. I want so much for you to find that abundant life in Me. Come, won't you allow Me to show you?

But the father said to his servants, 'Quick! Bring the best robe and put it on him. Put a ring on his finger and sandals on his feet. Bring the fattened calf and kill it. Let's have a feast and celebrate. For this son of mine was dead and is alive again; he was lost and is found.' So they began to celebrate.

—Luke 15:22-24

JANUARY 12

*H*ow do you see Me? Do you see Me as a strict, unfeeling judge who is going to give you a list of things to do in order to please Me? That is not My nature. I didn't come to judge you as a person. I came to judge the sin and remove it from your life. I also came to reveal to you your purpose…to release destiny into you…to release truth over you…to show you who you are now, as a new creation and as My heir! I have no list of chores for you to do. It is out of a love relationship with Me that you will do mighty and wonderful things that will be pleasing to Me. It is your choice though what you do or don't do in My name. I will love you regardless because My love is not based on what you do, but on what My Son did. My love for you will not change and can't get any deeper.

The Lord is not slow in keeping his promise, as some understand slowness. Instead he is patient with you, not wanting anyone to perish, but everyone to come to repentance.
—2 Peter 3:9

Who is a God like you, who pardons sin and forgives the transgression of the remnant of his inheritance? You do not stay angry forever but delight to show mercy. You will again have compassion on us; you will tread our sins underfoot and hurl all our iniquities into the depths of the sea.
—Micah 7:18-19

JANUARY 13

I am a loving God. When I see you doing something that brings Me sorrow, I will let you know. But I never reveal it in a condemning, hurtful way. No, My ways are gentle and kind because I care that much about you and want My best for your life. As I show you a better way, I stay right there with you. If you stumble or find it difficult, I am there encouraging you and guiding you. You have My grace, which is My ability flowing through you for those times when you find it impossible to do things on your own strength. I desire for your heart to be opened to My perfect love and My perfect ways.

I am the true vine, and my Father is the gardener. He cuts off every branch in me that bears no fruit, while every branch that does bear fruit he prunes so that it will be even more fruitful.
—John 15:1-2

Very truly I tell you, unless a kernel of wheat falls to the ground and dies, it remains only a single seed. But if it dies, it produces many seeds. —John 12:24

When you feel like you are walking in darkness, alone, frightened or lost, consciously stop that thought and remember I am here. I am right here with you, even when you don't feel or are aware of My presence. It is at these times I encourage you to stop looking at the darkness and look to Me. Turn your focus away from what you are going through and focus on Me and what I can give you. I am the sovereign Lord who is in control of everything! I created everything. I am the source of everything, and I happen to love you very much. The world gives you sorrow, pain and discouragement, but I give you peace, strength and hope! Come to Me, My child, and let Me help.

And the God of all grace, who called you to his eternal glory in Christ, after you have suffered a little while, will himself restore you and make you strong, firm and steadfast.

—1 Peter 5:10

Blessed is the one who perseveres under trial because, having stood the test, that person will receive the crown of life that the Lord has promised to those who love him.

—James 1:12

How often do you try to exceed expectations at home, work, at church, with your appearance, or in countless other ways? You have the expectation that in order to be acceptable, you have to measure up to standards so high they are unattainable. This leads to stress and frustration. Perfectionism is an unattainable goal, a lie. I have not put this burden on you. Please stop striving for something that cannot be attained and rest in Me. Learn from the example in My Word, where Martha was upset as she prepared for My Son's visit. She fretted about everything being perfect and missed the opportunity to sit at My Son's feet and rest as her sister, Mary did. Mary chose the better way which was My perfect way! Won't you make the choice to stop striving and rest in Me?

But Martha was distracted by all the preparations that had to be made. She came to him and asked, "Lord, don't you care that my sister has left me to do the work by myself? Tell her to help me!" "Martha, Martha," the Lord answered, "you are worried and upset about many things, but few things are needed or indeed only one. Mary has chosen what is better, and it will not be taken away from her."

—Luke 10:40-42

JANUARY 16

I know you see with your eyes what mankind is doing and all the unfairness and injustice. You feel like no one seems to care or be concerned or is really doing anything about it. I know you want results now, and it tears you apart that nothing seems to be happening. My child, I see what you see, and it grieves Me, too. This is not My doing but sin that entered the world. Take your focus off what you are seeing and be in prayer. This is the most important thing you can do! I'm asking you to be still before Me and to put your hope in Me. Trust in Me and see what I will do! It may not be your way, but it is the perfect way. Being in My presence and experiencing My love and blessing are great rewards.

Be still before the Lord and wait patiently for him; do not fret when people succeed in their ways, when they carry out their wicked schemes.

—Psalm 37:7

JANUARY 17

I know you may sometimes feel I am nowhere near and have abandoned and forgotten about you. Please don't go by your feelings, for these are lies. I would never leave you. You wrestle with negative thoughts that just don't stop, and sometimes they feel relentless. I watch with sorrow as I see this. It grieves My heart to see you this way. My dear one, come to Me and spend time with Me and get to know Me better. Learn about Me in My word and allow Me to love you, to share with you a better way! I love you more than you can imagine and desire a relationship with you.

The Lord is close to the brokenhearted and saves those who are crushed in spirit.

—Psalm 34:18

But I trust in your unfailing love; my heart rejoices in your salvation.

—Psalm 13:5

JANUARY 18

I am your rock and fortress and a safe place to dwell. I am the shield that protects you. I undergird you to keep you steady and freely give you My strength. Write these truths on your heart. Remember them when you are going through rough times, when deep waters of grief swirl all around you, when people hurt you and mistreat you, when crises arise; I am there to rescue you, pull you out of the raging storm and set you down in a place of peace. You have these promises always. They are in My Word. Why do I do this for you? Because I love you so much, and that is My heart.

My salvation and my honor depend on God; he is my mighty rock, my refuge.
—Psalm 62:7

My God is my rock, in whom I take refuge, my shield and the horn of my salvation.
He is my stronghold, my refuge and my savior— from violent people you save me.
—2 Samuel 22:3

JANUARY 19

*C*ome, learn from Me and let Me show you My ways and how I do things. I want to show you how to live life abundantly and not to just get by or just get through each day. You don't have to just settle or be resigned to the way things are. There is a huge difference, and I want to guide you to the better way. Come, take My hand, and walk with Me. Watch what I do and hear what I say. I will guide your every step. I know what will bring you harm, and I will point those places out so you can choose not to go down that path. Get to know Me better so you will be able to trust Me. Will you place your hope in Me?

Show me your ways, Lord, teach me your paths. Guide me in your truth and
teach me, for you are God my Savior, and my hope is in you all day long. Remember,
Lord, your great mercy and love, for they are from of old.
—Psalm 25:4-6

For this God is our God for ever and ever; he will be our guide even to the end.
—Psalm 48:14

I hear your cries. Sometimes I don't answer right away because I care about a heart change and want the best for you. A heart change is long-lasting and is vital for living a life for Me. If I would just answer you right away, that wouldn't really change anything. The next time you are in the same or a similar situation, you would be in despair again rather than having learned how to avoid the problem or how to handle it and what to do. I will give you a new song, as a new way of handling any situation that arises! Turn to Me and keep your focus there as I help you through the storm you are facing. Will you trust Me, My child, and learn from Me?

I will sprinkle clean water on you, and you will be clean; I will cleanse you from all your impurities and from all your idols. I will give you a new heart and put a new spirit in you; I will remove from you your heart of stone and give you a heart of flesh. And I will put my Spirit in you and move you to follow my decrees and be careful to keep my laws.
—Ezekiel 36:25-27

Create in me a pure heart, O God, and renew a steadfast spirit within me.
—Psalm 51:10

*D*o you have any idea how much I love you? I love you with an everlasting love that is endlessly deep, wide and long. You cannot fathom the depth of My love for you. Even though you are not perfect, I love you. Even when you have a bad day or make bad choices, I love you. Even when you turn your back on Me, I love you. Even when you take My name in vain, I love you. I created you and thought of every little detail in forming you. I made you because I wanted a relationship with you. Take down any barriers that are preventing you from coming to Me and receiving the love I want to give you, My dear child. I'm not going anywhere and will continue to pursue you, for you are of great value and worth to Me!

No, in all these things we are more than conquerors through him who loved us. For I am convinced that neither death nor life, neither angels nor demons, neither the present nor the future, nor any powers, neither height nor depth, nor anything else in all creation, will be able to separate us from the love of God that is in Christ Jesus our Lord.
—Romans 8:37-39

The Lord appeared to us in the past, saying: "I have loved you with an everlasting love; I have drawn you with unfailing kindness."
—Jeremiah 31:3

I love you, My child. When I see you wanting to spend time with Me, I come to you right away. Even though the prayers of the entire world continue to come up to Me in My throne room, I come to you. I can do that because I am Almighty God. I don't have the same restrictions as you. I can be in all places at all times. I created you to have a relationship with Me. I come running to you when I see you come running to Me. I embrace you with a love that only your Heavenly Father can give. It is a love with no strings or restrictions and is there forevermore. It gives Me joy when you want to spend time together. I am Almighty God, who desires a continual relationship with you.

And surely I am with you always, to the very end of the age.

—Matthew 28:20b

Here I am! I stand at the door and knock. If anyone hears my voice and opens the door, I will come in and eat with that person, and they with me.

—Revelation 3:20

D o you know that I speak to you? I speak to you constantly, for how could I not? You're My child whom I absolutely adore! I speak to you in soft whispers or thoughts. I speak to you through friends and through praise songs and hymns. I speak to you through the Bible. I speak to you in the silence… Let go of any lies telling you differently and any barriers that prevent you from hearing Me. I give you special hearing through spiritual ears. The more you intentionally use these spiritual ears that I have given you, you will hear Me more and more, and in return, will be so blessed! Listen, I'm speaking to you now…

My sheep listen to my voice; I know them, and they follow me. I give them eternal life, and they shall never perish; no one will snatch them out of my hand.

—John 10:27-28

'Call to me and I will answer you and tell you great and unsearchable things you do not know.'

—Jeremiah 33:3

When you are going through a trial that may have no end in sight and you are aware that you are becoming exhausted, pause a moment and ask yourself if you have given this problem to Me. Have you forgotten I am right by your side waiting for you to bring Me into the situation by calling out My name? I am the everlasting God and have created everything. I know everything about the situation and see the whole picture from beginning to end. I never grow weary or weak but have endless power and strength! I pour these things into you daily to give you renewed strength. I give not just energy but a fresh, renewed outlook. I give you strength to soar above the situation and to run and persevere to the very end. So come to Me, and place your hope and trust in Me!

Do you not know? Have you not heard? The Lord is the everlasting God, the Creator of the ends of the earth. He will not grow tired or weary, and his understanding no one can fathom. He gives strength to the weary and increases the power of the weak. Even youths grow tired and weary, and young men stumble and fall; but those who hope in the Lord will renew their strength. They will soar on wings like eagles; they will run and not grow weary, they will walk and not be faint.

—Isaiah 40:28-31

JANUARY 25

I take great delight when you are worshiping Me. I really do inhabit your praises. I love when you worship Me in spirit and in truth, with total abandonment. Come, let your guard down and worship Me like you've never done before. Draw Me into your heart. Yes, draw Me close to your heart. Take your time and enjoy the journey. The fragrance of your worship draws Me in. You will know when that happens. I can't wait for you to have this experience and to repeat it over and over again. When you're in My presence, you aren't thinking at all about your problems because your full focus is on Me and who I am. Come, draw Me into your heart right now!

Blessed are those who have learned to acclaim you, who walk in the light of your presence, Lord.

—Psalm 89:15

Yet a time is coming and has now come when the true worshipers will worship the Father in the Spirit and in truth, for they are the kind of worshipers the Father seeks.

—John 4:23

*I*n the silence you can find Me. Turn off the noise of the world and the thoughts in your mind. Come to a place where time stands still, and there you will find Me. Let Me teach you how to communicate with no words being exchanged. Feel My presence fill up the room. Intentionally awaken your spiritual senses to feel My touch and to see Me. I want you to hear My voice, to smell My fragrance, and to taste and see how good I am! Sometimes it takes practice and patience in using these special senses that I have given you. You really can experience Me in ways you hadn't thought possible by using any of these senses. Try it, press in and persevere. Best of all, you will experience My love in a whole new way.

Taste and see that the Lord is good, blessed is the one who takes refuge in him.
—Psalm 34:8

*He says, "Be still, and know that I am God; I will be
exalted among the nations, I will be exalted in the earth."*
—Psalm 46:10

JANUARY 27

*S*ometimes it is hard to relate to Me as Abba Father, your Heavenly Daddy. Your biological father may not have been loving. You may have been hurt or rejected by someone you thought loved you. Don't confuse Me with your earthly father or anyone else in your life. My ways are always loving, gentle and kind. That is My nature! I could not be anything else to you. My ways give you encouragement. I see the potential in you and call it out! I build you up. I cheer you on. I give you hope and a future.

*Yet to all who did receive him, to those who believed in his name,
he gave the right to become children of God- children born not of natural descent,
nor of human decision or a husband's will, but born of God.*
—John 1:12-13

*See what great love the Father has lavished on us, that we should be called children of God!
And that is what we are! The reason the world does not know us is that it did not know him.*
—1 John 3:1

I have given you one of My most prized possessions, My Word, the living Bible! In it are pages upon pages of treasures to help you, to encourage you, and to inform you. It is the handbook on life and has everything in there that you need! There is no error in My Word which may be hard for you to understand, but it is true. My Word reveals how I think, who I am and what I have done for you. It is rich in history, in meaning and insight. There may be things that you may not understand or have trouble agreeing with. That's okay; hold on to your questions. Some will be answered at another point in time and others you just have to trust Me. As you get to know Me better through My Word and time spent with Me, trusting Me will become easier. I want you to treasure what I prize so highly. Will you do that?

All Scripture is God-breathed and is useful for teaching,
rebuking, correcting and training in righteousness.

—2 Timothy 3:16

And we also thank God continually because, when you received the word of God,
which you heard from us, you accepted it not as a human word, but as it actually is,
the word of God, which is indeed at work in you who believe.

—1 Thessalonians 2:13

JANUARY 29

I know you want to read the Bible because you know how important it is to Me that you do. I am grateful that you want to honor that. But I also know, if you are honest, you sometimes don't really want to read it. You may also have trouble understanding portions. You may even wonder how this relates to your life and what you can learn from it. I don't look down on you when you feel this way. What I want to do is help you and encourage you. Ask Me to give you a hunger for My Word. Ask Me to give you insight. I will gladly answer you. Listen also to the answers I give you through other people, through your thoughts, through other verses from My Word. Keep persevering; you won't regret it.

My Word that goes out from my mouth: It will not return to me empty,
but will accomplish what I desire and achieve the purpose for which I sent it.

—Isaiah 55:11

For everything that was written in the past was written to teach us, so that through the
endurance taught in the Scriptures and the encouragement they provide we might have hope.

—Romans 15:4

*C*ome, abide in Me. As you live within this place of abiding, you will be immersed in My perfect love and in My glory. It is a wonderful place to be and to remain. Come, feel My contentment, peace and security as your mind and heart are focused only on intimacy with Me. As you remain in My presence, feel My strength and comfort being poured into you and where nothing else you are dealing with in life matters—only beholding My glory! It is a place you will long to stay once you have experienced it. It is here My promises to you become more real as faith and trust in Me are strengthened. Oh, won't you come and abide?

Remain in me, as I also remain in you. No branch can bear fruit by itself; it must remain in the vine. Neither can you bear fruit unless you remain in me. I am the vine; you are the branches. If you remain in me and I in you, you will bear much fruit; apart from me you can do nothing.
—John 15:4-5

He who dwells in the shelter of the Most High, will abide in the shadow of the Almighty.
—Psalm 91:1 (NASB)

*D*o not be concerned where you will spend eternity if you know Me as your Savior. There are many rooms in My house that I have prepared for My children. You will love it here! I will come for you so that you can spend forever with Me here in My home. There will come that day when you will be able to see Me and spend time with Me in the way you long for. You probably think about eternity from time to time and may even have some fear, knowing but not knowing what is to come or even being sure where you will be. That is okay. It is at those times of wondering that I want you to remember what My Word says. You will be with Me forever in My home if you know Jesus as your Savior.

My Father's house has many rooms; if that were not so, would I have told you that I am going there to prepare a place for you? And if I go and prepare a place for you, I will come back and take you to be with me that you also may be where I am.
—John 14:2-3

For God so loved the world that he gave his one and only Son that whoever believes in him shall not perish but have eternal life.
—John 3:16

FEBRUARY 1

*Y*ou have suffered an unimaginable loss and are grieving. You can't imagine life without your loved one. Your heart aches for what you can't hold anymore. My child, I grieve with you… Please allow Me into your heart. Let Me hold you in My loving arms close to My heart. Feel My love and peace slowly fill the emptiness. I will walk alongside of you continuing to pour into you endless supplies of strength, comfort and peace that only I can give. My child I love you, come to Me.

Blessed are those who mourn, for they will be comforted.

—Matthew 5:4

He heals the brokenhearted and binds up their wounds.

—Psalm 147:3

FEBRUARY 2

I want you to thirst for Me, to really, truly thirst for Me so that nothing else but knowing Me will quench that thirst. I want you to be like the deer that drink hungrily in the stream. They pant for that water, and nothing else is on their minds but the water that takes care of their thirst and is long-lasting. I want you to be like the deer, where nothing else in all the world can satisfy you as I can. I desire for you to come searching for Me, knowing I am the only one who can completely quench your thirst. Will you come to Me and be satisfied?

As the deer pants for streams of water, so my soul pants for you, my God.
My soul thirsts for God, for the living God. When can I go and meet with God?

—Psalm 42:1-2

My heart says of you, "Seek his face!" Your face, Lord, I will seek.

—Psalm 27:8

FEBRUARY 3

*Y*ou may be hesitant to call Me Daddy, thinking it is disrespectful. I am Almighty God, but I want you to also know Me as your Daddy. After all, you are My child whom I dearly love! When you come to know Me well, you will start to think of Me as your Daddy. You will know how much I love you and want to spend time with you. When you call Me Daddy after experiencing My love for you, I will know your heart and that you are calling Me Daddy with respect, honor and most of all, with the love of a dearly loved child! My child, I am your Heavenly Daddy, and I love when you call Me Daddy!

The Spirit you received does not make you slaves, so that you live in fear again; rather, the Spirit you received brought about your adoption to sonship. And by him we cry, "Abba, Father."
—Romans 8:15

And, "I will be a Father to you, and you will be my sons and daughters, says the Lord Almighty."
—2 Corinthians 6:18

FEBRUARY 4

I want to be the smile on your face and the song in your heart! This will only happen as you connect to Me constantly throughout your day-to-day life. When you are a part of Me, you can't help but smile, for your thoughts won't be on your daily life with all its challenges. Instead, your whole being will be focused on Me and being in My presence! It is there you will find My peace and comfort, My warmth, and, most of all, My love. You will want to stay there because it really is a happy and wonderful place to be, and it will put a song in your heart!

He put a new song in my mouth, a hymn of praise to our God.
Many will see and fear the Lord and put their trust in him.
—Psalm 40:3

A happy heart makes the face cheerful, but heartache crushes the spirit.
—Proverbs 15:13

FEBRUARY 5

I want the best for you. I am your biggest cheerleader! I watch you not with anticipation of failure but with the expectation of victory. I see your potential. I see the whole picture and know the ending. I give you everything you need to succeed. Don't let doubts or lies get in the way. Push past fear and negativity. I am there by your side, encouraging you and guiding you with every step you take. Please be aware of that. Having Me cheering you on and being right by your side make all the difference in the world!

And my God will meet all your needs according to the riches of his glory in Christ Jesus.
—Philippians 4:19

His divine power has given us everything we need for a godly life
through our knowledge of him who called us by his own glory and goodness.
—2 Peter 1:3

FEBRUARY 6

*P*eople are watching your life. They are watching what you say and do, how you handle yourself and how you react and respond to situations. Are you aware of that? You are here for a purpose. Your life has meaning. You leave a mark on other people's lives. Are you living for Me? Will what they observe be something for them to emulate? At the end of your life, how will people remember you? Will they remember you for what you did for a living or by how you made them feel? Will they see Me in the way you live your life?

Therefore, I urge you, brothers and sisters, in view of God's mercy, to offer your bodies as a living sacrifice, holy and pleasing to God—this is your true and proper worship. Do not conform to the pattern of this world, but be transformed by the renewing of your mind. Then you will be able to test and approve what God's will is—his good, pleasing and perfect will.
—Romans 12:1-2

*Y*ou need a Savior, for all have sinned, but My Son died for just that reason. My love for you is that great! If you believe that Jesus is your Savior, everything He did for you is yours! Every single one of your sins—past, present and future—were nailed to the cross when He died. On the cross, Jesus exchanged your sin for His perfect righteousness so that when I look at you, I don't see any sin, only My Son in you! Jesus died to give you life. Your sins were cleansed and washed away by His blood, and I remember them no more. You have been made righteous in My sight! I know that is hard to comprehend. Step into what has already been done for you and believe it.

God made him who had no sin to be sin for us,
so that in him we might become the righteousness of God.
—2 Corinthians 5:21

If you declare with your mouth, "Jesus is Lord," and believe in your heart
that God raised him from the dead, you will be saved. For it is with your heart that you believe
and are justified, and it is with your mouth that you profess your faith and are saved.
—Romans 10:9-10

*W*hy are you here? Did you ever think about why I made you exactly as I made you? Why I gave you the personality you have or the interests, passions, and gifts you have? Why I gave you the parents I gave you or raised you in the community I placed you in? All have meaning. Even the bad situations of your life have purpose. I can use you mightily if you are willing. In the bad situations, learn from Me how to face them and walk through them. I walk with you, helping you to find victory over them and, in the process, develop your character to handle whatever comes your way. Did you ever think of it that way? Embrace your history and the opportunities it places in your path.

In him we were also chosen, having been predestined according to the plan of him
who works out everything in conformity with the purpose of his will, in order that we,
who were the first to put our hope in Christ, might be for the praise of his glory.
—Ephesians 1:11-12

*C*ome, see My streams of living water spring forth from My eternal love. Be refreshed and filled! It will quench your thirst. Bathe in it and be cleansed. Drink of it and thirst no more. Stand under the fountain of water and be revived. Partake of My living water from the new heart that I have given you. You will be so blessed. Be completely filled, and then turn your focus to others. Go and pour out this living water on them, bringing My life and light to those you touch. Keep repeating the cycle of getting filled up and then pouring out. You will be so blessed.

Jesus answered her, "If you knew the gift of God and who it is that asks you for a drink, you would have asked him and he would have given you living water."

—John 4:10

On the last and greatest day of the festival, Jesus stood and said in a loud voice, "Let anyone who is thirsty come to me and drink. Whoever believes in me, as Scripture has said, rivers of living water will flow from within them." By this he meant the Spirit, whom those who believed in him were later to receive. Up to that time the Spirit had not been given, since Jesus had not yet been glorified.

—John 7:37-39

FEBRUARY 10

*R*un the race with endurance by focusing on Me. I am cheering you on. When you are weak, I give you strength. When you want to give up, I am right by your side holding your hand. When you lose focus, look into My eyes. When you start to doubt, recall My Word. Fight the good fight and finish the course. Lay aside every weight and sin which cling so closely. It is work, but press on to the worthy goal. Remember, I am your greatest encourager and My Son died so that you are able to finish strong.

I press on toward the goal to win the prize for which God has called me heavenward in Christ Jesus.

—Philippians 3:14

I have fought the good fight, I have finished the race, I have kept the faith.

—2 Timothy 4:7

FEBRUARY 11

$\mathcal{T}$here is a great cloud of witnesses surrounding you! They are your example, and they are cheering you on to the finish line! Lay aside anything holding you back and get rid of anything weighing you down. Once you let go of the stuff, you will run the race with more ease and endurance. Fix your eyes on Me, for I am your prize and goal—your pure joy! Look forward to the goal so you don't lose heart or grow weary. Pace yourself, for it is a marathon. Replenish yourself with My sustenance. All those who have gone on before you cheer on either side, and I am right there at the finish line waiting for you with open arms!

Therefore, since we are surrounded by such a great cloud of witnesses,
let us throw off everything that hinders and the sin that so easily entangles. And
let us run with perseverance the race marked out for us, fixing our eyes on Jesus, the
pioneer and perfecter of faith. For the joy set before him he endured the cross, scorning
its shame, and sat down at the right hand of the throne of God. Consider him who endured
such opposition from sinners, so that you will not grow weary and lose heart.
—Hebrews 12:1-3

FEBRUARY 12

$\mathcal{I}$ invite you to come closer to Me, to press in for a deeper relationship which I want so much for you to have. When you align yourself with Me, your heart will mesh with My heart and you will hear them beating in sync. That is true intimacy. As we work together with a common goal, you will know Me so well and can anticipate My lead and follow it without missing a beat. I love when you press in, and keep pressing in. When we line up, My will becomes your will. I will give you the desires of your heart because it is then that your heart desires what Mine does. Oh, won't you come closer and experience this intimacy!

You, God, are my God, earnestly I seek you; I thirst for you, my whole being longs for you,
in a dry and parched land where there is no water. I have seen you in the sanctuary and
beheld your power and your glory. Because your love is better than life, my lips will glorify
you. I will praise you as long as I live, and in your name I will lift up my hands.
—Psalm 63:1-4

*T*here are times in your life when you find yourself estranged from someone and the heartache is very real. The relationship may be salvageable. It is at these times I want you to look humbly and deeply into yourself. Is there something you might have done contributing to the break? Ask Me if you really don't know. Ask Me with a teachable heart and I will answer. Do whatever you can to be the peacemaker. Reach out in love and with a sincere heart. Pray a blessing over them. Allow time for a healing to take place. If nothing happens, continue to pray a blessing on them. Guard your mind and don't entertain any thoughts that would hinder a reconciliation. Keep the door open always.

Blessed are the peacemakers, for they will be called children of God.
—Matthew 5:9

If it is possible, as far as it depends on you, live at peace with everyone.
—Romans 12:18

FEBRUARY 14

*T*oday is Valentine's Day. It's a day the world sets aside to focus on those you love and who are dear to you. On this day you especially show kindness, patience, and love, and you do special things to show the person how you feel about them. This pleases Me that you show this goodness. But what about the other days of the year? I encourage you to show this same kindness year round. Be quick to hear, slow to speak, and slow to anger. Don't insist on being right or wanting your own way. Resist being envious, irritable, or resentful. Do not keep score or hold on to grudges. Don't point out the faults of your loved one. I know you think this is hard to do, and you're right; on your own strength it is impossible. But you have My grace, which is My ability flowing through you. Depend on Me and love like I love every day of the year.

Love is patient, love is kind. It does not envy, it does not boast, it is not proud. It does not dishonor others, it is not self-seeking, it is not easily angered, it keeps no record of wrongs.
—1 Corinthians 13:4-5

My dear brothers and sisters, take note of this: Everyone should be quick to listen, slow to speak and slow to become angry.
—James 1:19

FEBRUARY 15

I want you to empty out your heart. Empty it of all the things that get in the way of what I want to give you. Open your heart up to what I want to pour into it. I want to fill you with things that bring life, light, and joy to you. Have a teachable heart and one that is open to correction, learning, and training. Give Me your yielded heart, one where the rest of you gets out of the way. Finally, give Me an obedient heart, a heart that says yes to Me without question. An obedient heart knows Me well and therefore has peace with being obedient. That is My desire for you.

I will give them an undivided heart and put a new spirit in them;
I will remove from them their heart of stone and give them a heart of flesh.
—Ezekiel 11:19

Create in me a pure heart, O God, and renew a steadfast spirit within me.
—Psalm 51:10

FEBRUARY 16

*C*ome, worship Me in spirit and in truth. Engage your whole heart and hold nothing back. I want to give you a real passion for Me. Get to know Me through My Word, and who I really am. Earnestly seek to know My nature and character, for it is then that your worship of Me will grow deeper. Oh, it's a wonderful place to be! I want you to experience true worship, for it is then that I will be truly glorified and you will be truly blessed. Will you let Me help you? All you need is a willing heart.

Yet a time is coming and has now come when the true worshipers will
worship the Father in the Spirit and in truth, for they are the kind of worshipers the
Father seeks. God is spirit, and his worshipers must worship in the Spirit and in truth.
—John 4:23-24

The Lord is near to all who call on him, to all who call on him in truth.
—Psalm 145:18

FEBRUARY 17

I want your worship. I want all of you. Please don't hold back. Lay aside everything that would hinder and get in the way. You say you love Me with all your heart, soul, mind and strength. But do you really? I'm not condemning you when I ask this. I ask this as a Father wanting His best for His children! When you look at your life, what do you see: total surrender or something else? Give Me your absolute love and surrender, and watch what happens…

*Love the Lord your God with all your heart and with all
your soul and with all your mind and with all your strength.*
—Mark 12:30

*Do not store up for yourselves treasures on earth, where moths and vermin destroy,
and where thieves break in and steal. But store up for yourselves treasures in heaven,
where moths and vermin do not destroy, and where thieves do not break in and steal.
For where your treasure is, there your heart will be also.*
—Matthew 6:19-21

FEBRUARY 18

*W*hen you are worshiping Me, My glory fills the room you are in. I will be standing right there with you, for I inhabit the praises of My children. Your eyes have been opened to see Me, but it is with your spiritual eyes that you will see Me, and this comes from your heart. Do not be discouraged if this doesn't happen right away or you aren't aware of it. But you will see, for I dearly want to reveal Myself to you. I long to interact with you in ways you have yet to experience. Come, look into My eyes and you will see what pure love looks like. As you look into My eyes, your problems won't seem so big because you will be seeing My greatness instead. This is just a taste of what I want to show you. Ask for more and I will gladly give you your heart's desire, for that is My heart's desire for you.

Let us go to his dwelling place, let us worship at his footstool.
—Psalm 132:7

Take delight in the Lord, and he will give you the desires of your heart.
—Psalm 37:4

$\mathcal{C}$all upon Me and you will find I am here, for you are never alone. Even when you don't "feel" My presence, that doesn't mean I'm not right by your side. When the waters close all around you and you lose hope, I am there. When you are overwhelmed or discouraged, I am there. I am there to give you strength when you feel like you can't go on. Come, turn to Me and don't walk this path alone. Walk with Me by your side.

The Lord replied, "My Presence will go with you, and I will give you rest.
—Exodus 33:14

You will seek me and find me when you seek me with all your heart.
—Jeremiah 29:13

$\mathcal{B}$ecause of sin in the world, there will be times when you will be hurt by people, even by loved ones and family. Sometimes it is intentional on their part, and sometimes they aren't even aware of the hurt they cause. Anger may well up inside you. You may even choose to replay the incident in your mind over and over again. That hurt, if left to itself, will lead to anger, bitterness, resentment and unforgiveness. This will eat away at you if you choose to allow it. Do not give the devil a foothold! Choose life by choosing to forgive. Choose to let go of the anger and hurt. By knowing My nature and character, you know I am there for you. I'm asking you to do something that I have equipped you for and have given you the power to overcome. The hardest part is for you to choose to let go of the hurt and anger. Once you make that choice, it becomes easier because it is My power in you that enables you to let go of the emotions. This will set you free! And you can breathe again.

And do not grieve the Holy Spirit of God, with whom you were sealed for the day of redemption. Get rid of all bitterness, rage and anger, brawling and slander, along with every form of malice. Be kind and compassionate to one another, forgiving each other, just as in Christ God forgave you.
—Ephesians 4:30-32

My dear brothers and sisters, take note of this: Everyone should be quick to listen, slow to speak and slow to become angry, because human anger does not produce the righteousness that God desires.
—James 1:19-20

I am your cornerstone, your rock, fortress, under-girder and the only constant in your life. I am unchanging and always by your side. I give you strength when you are weak. I guide your path when you don't know where to turn. I fill you up when you have nothing left. I am your comfort in the midst of the storm. Worries vanish when you are in My presence. When sickness comes, I am your healer. I forgive and redeem you when you make mistakes. All guilt and shame must vanish by My name. I am your everything! Come and worship Me in spirit and in truth.

Worship the Lord your God, and his blessing will be on your food and water.
I will take away sickness from among you.
—Exodus 23:25

Do not tremble, do not be afraid. Did I not proclaim this and foretell it long ago?
You are my witnesses. Is there any God besides me? No, there is no other Rock; I know not one.
—Isaiah 44:8

FEBRUARY 22

I formed you inside your mother's womb. I created you with a unique personality and features that only you possess. You are My masterpiece and made to perfection in My eyes. You are made in My image. Do you realize how special that makes you? You were shaped by all of your experiences too. Whether they were good or bad, it helped form who you are now. All the pruning I do, I do with love. All of this is a building stone for the calling I have on your life. It is a high calling! I am so proud of you for stepping into that calling. Let Me show you what I have equipped you for and so lovingly prepared for you to do. You will be so blessed!

For we are God's handiwork, created in Christ Jesus to do
good works, which God prepared in advance for us to do.
—Ephesians 2:10

Yet you, Lord, are our Father. We are the clay, you are the potter; we are all the work of your hand.
—Isaiah 64:8

FEBRUARY 23

*T*hroughout your life, you will experience anger. Anger in itself is not sinful. It is an emotion I have given you. Some anger is good when it is directed at injustice, sin and evil. It's what you do with that anger that can lead to sin. When you keep ahold of it and replay the experience in your mind, that will only lead you down a path I don't want you to take. Let My Word help you and save you from the horrid effects of anger. You can let go of the anger for you have My power! You have the same power that raised Jesus from the dead inside of you right now. I will help you in letting it go if you make that choice. Please choose the better way!

In your anger do not sin. Do not let the sun go down while
you are still angry, and do not give the devil a foothold.
—Ephesians 4:26-27

A person's wisdom yields patience; it is to one's glory to overlook an offense.
—Proverbs 19:11

FEBRUARY 24

I'm calling you to walk on water! I'm calling you to do the impossible! According to the world's eyes, it can't be done. The world doesn't know Me, but you do. Your immediate reaction is, "Lord, I can't." You are right. You can't, but I CAN! I am calling you to stop looking at the situation that is paralyzing you and causing you great distress. Fix your eyes on Me and never look back. You will be tempted to look back but stay steadfast and gaze into My eyes. Take My hand that I am extending to you and walk with Me. I know, the first step is the hardest and it takes great faith. But your faith is rooted in knowing who I AM. Come, walk on water with Me…

Shortly before dawn Jesus went out to them, walking on the lake. When the disciples
saw him walking on the lake, they were terrified. "It's a ghost," they said, and cried out in fear.
But Jesus immediately said to them: "Take courage! It is I. Don't be afraid." "Lord, if it's you,"
Peter replied, "tell me to come to you on the water." "Come," he said. Then Peter got down
out of the boat, walked on the water and came toward Jesus. But when he saw the
wind, he was afraid and, beginning to sink, cried out, "Lord, save me!" Immediately Jesus
reached out his hand and caught him. "You of little faith," he said, "why did you doubt?"
—Matthew 14:25-31

FEBRUARY 25

When you wake up in the morning where do your thoughts take you? Are you thinking about the lack of sleep you got, about all the things you have to do today, or about the situation you face? When you focus on things of this world, they only weigh you down. My child, let Me show you a better way. No matter what is going on in your life, begin each morning with thanksgiving. Think of all you are grateful for and give thanks to Me. Acknowledge who I am to you and give thanks. Watch for My hand in everything you are facing and for My goodness being displayed throughout the day. Focus on the positive and constantly reject negative thoughts. Keep that as your focus. Watch how your life and attitude will change.

A cheerful heart is good medicine, but a crushed spirit dries up the bones.

—Proverbs 17:22

The thief comes only to steal and kill and destroy;
I have come that they may have life, and have it to the full.

—John 10:10

FEBRUARY 26

Your heart is the essence of who you are. It is the part of you that connects with Me and is the source of everything in your life. What you think, say and do flows from there. It is the wellspring of your life. It is also under constant attack by the lies you believe. Those lies can threaten your health, relationships, job and even your legacy. That is why I want you to realize how important it is to guard your heart. I care about you so much and want you to be diligent about guarding it. The key is to become aware of what you are thinking. If your thoughts are not rooted in Me, cast them out and keep casting them out as they rear their ugly heads again and again. Hold fast to My word and to My ways. I empower you to do this!

Above all else, guard your heart, for everything you do flows from it.

—Proverbs 4:23

Do not be anxious about anything, but in every situation, by prayer and petition,
with thanksgiving,present your requests to God. And the peace of God, which transcends
all understanding, will guard your hearts and your minds in Christ Jesus.

—Philippians 4:6-7

*I*know sometimes you feel lost and all alone, as if no one really cares what happens to you or what you are going through. You feel as if there is no one there to offer support or help. You are discouraged, and each day it seems to get worse. My child, you are not alone! That is a lie that you are believing. My Son, Jesus, is right next to Me, interceding on your behalf. He is your biggest encourager and that's not all. The Holy Spirit is also next to Me, speaking on your behalf. It doesn't get better than that. Even though you won't see this with your earthly eyes, it is happening and without ceasing. Write this on your heart. Draw strength from this and be encouraged!

In the same way, the Spirit helps us in our weakness. We do not know what
we ought to pray for, but the Spirit himself intercedes for us through wordless groans.
—Romans 8:26

Who then is the one who condemns? No one. Christ Jesus who died—more than that, who was
raised to life—is at the right hand of God and is also interceding for us.
—Romans 8:34

*I*have given you a heart transplant. You no longer have the heart you were born with. You are a new creation and with that comes a new heart, a heart that is rooted in My love. It is a heart that looks at people the way I do and that loves people with My love. Let go of operating from your old self and surrender it. Then connect to Me and let My love pour out from you to others. As you connect, you begin to see people the way I do. You will see that they have been wounded and are hurting. It is out of that wounded state that they repeat the cycle. You have a choice. Allow My love to be what you and others feel!

But the Lord said to Samuel, "Do not consider his appearance or his height,
for I have rejected him. The Lord does not look at the things people look at. People
look at the outward appearance, but the Lord looks at the heart."
—1 Samuel 16:7

Be kind and compassionate to one another, forgiving each other, just as in Christ God forgave you.
—Ephesians 4:32

*M*y cross brings you life—eternal life in My presence. But until that glorious day, it gives you abundant life for the present. No more do you have to carry the burdens you've been carrying, for they have all been nailed to the cross. When Jesus died, these burdens died too and are buried. When Jesus rose again, He conquered death and all these things you worry about. The same power that raised Him is in you. He died to set you free! Let go of the lies you are believing. All the things weighing you down are gone, for they do not need to have control over you. You have the victory! Awaken to this reality. Renew your mind, write it on your heart and be set free.

The thief comes only to steal and kill and destroy;
I have come that they may have life, and have it to the full.

—John 10:10

May the God of hope fill you with all joy and peace as you trust in him,
so that you may overflow with hope by the power of the Holy Spirit.

—Romans 15:13

*S*atan is real and does exist. He tempts and accuses you and tries to be in control. He fills your mind with lies that are subtle, deceptive and believable. He watches you and looks for your vulnerabilities. He is deceitful. But the good news is, I am all powerful and he doesn't even come close to that! He has already been defeated and does not have to control you. You have everything you need in Me. You do not need to fear the defeated enemy. Put on your armor. Renew your mind in who I am and keep your focus on Me. Don't give him any of your attention. Walk in the victory I have already given you.

Therefore put on the full armor of God, so that when the day of evil comes, you may be able to
stand your ground, and after you have done everything, to stand. Stand firm then, with the
belt of truth buckled around your waist, with the breastplate of righteousness in place, and
with your feet fitted with the readiness that comes from the gospel of peace. In addition to
all this, take up the shield of faith, with which you can extinguish all the flaming arrows of the
evil one. Take the helmet of salvation and the sword of the Spirit, which is the word of God.

—Ephesians 6:13-17

MARCH 3

I want the best for you. My will is good, pleasing and perfect. Sometimes it doesn't feel that way to you. Sometimes you can't even begin to see anything good or you are in the desert and can't feel My presence. But remember, My thoughts and ways of doing things are different from yours. Sometimes you just need to trust Me. You can do that more easily if you already know My nature and character, so keep pressing in to know Me and read My Word. I am more interested in your character than your comfort. That may sound harsh to you, but I do all things for a good reason. Sometimes My plan for you is often uncovered in a desert situation. Sometimes I am changing you from the inside, so you are better able to handle life's challenges. Start seeking the good, pleasing and perfect in My will.

Do not conform to the pattern of this world, but be transformed by the renewing of your mind.
Then you will be able to test and approve what God's will is—his good, pleasing and perfect will.
—Romans 12:2

Not only so, but we also glory in our sufferings, because we know
that suffering produces perseverance; perseverance, character; and character, hope.
—Romans 5:3-4

MARCH 4

I want your all! I want you to love Me with all your heart, soul, mind and strength. You do that by surrendering your life to Me and by putting Me first in all you do. I don't care about rules and regulations, for they are carried out by obligation and don't truly come from the heart. I want your heart. I want a love relationship with you. I want you to hunger and thirst for more of Me. Come spend time with Me by sitting at My feet, letting Me hold you on My lap or walking side by side with Me. It is out of this precious time and this love relationship that everything else flows. Once you experience it, you will want more.

Love the Lord your God with all your heart and with all your soul and with all your strength.
—Deuteronomy 6:5

My soul yearns for you in the night; in the morning my spirit longs for you.
When your judgments come upon the earth, the people of the world learn righteousness.
—Isaiah 26:9

*W*hat do you value or spend most of your free time doing? Where do your day-dreams take you? Is it of earthly things that won't last? Or is it of heavenly things that will last for eternity? Anything you do for Me is a permanent treasure! A thankless job or a job that no one else sees you do is priceless in My eyes! Loving on My people who are My creation is worthy of My blessing. Whatever you do unto Me with joy in your heart I delight in. Where does your heart take you? Does it seek things that are pleasing to Me or a fleeting pleasure? Pause and look at your life. Where are your treasures stored?

Command them to do good, to be rich in good deeds, and to be generous and willing to share. In this way they will lay up treasure for themselves as a firm foundation for the coming age, so that they may take hold of the life that is truly life.
—1 Timothy 6:18

*S*ometimes you look at another person and wish you were more like them. You wish you could do what they are good at doing or wish you had the same person-ality. Please don't compare yourself to others. Guard your thought life. It doesn't matter in My eyes if someone is more talented in an area or can do something better. That's not what I look at. I look at your heart. Are you living for Me? Are you spending time in My presence? Remember, I created you and gave you the gifts and abilities that I wanted you to have. Be content and satisfied with how I made you, and use what I gave you for My glory!

Each one should test their own actions. Then they can take pride in themselves alone, without comparing themselves to someone else.
—Galatians 6:4

Am I now trying to win the approval of human beings, or of God? Or am I trying to please people? If I were still trying to please people, I would not be a servant of Christ.
—Galatians 1:10

MARCH 7

*Y*ou are a carrier of My love. I have poured My love into you and I want you to give it away. I want you to love people whether you like them or not, whether you agree with them or not; even if their appearance isn't pleasing to your sight, I want you to love them. Every single one of My creations has a heart and soul and has feelings and emotions just like you do. Be the person that reflects My image to them. Touch their lives as I have touched yours, and love them because I love them.

A new command I give you: Love one another. As I have loved you, so you must love one another.
—John 13:34

We love because he first loved us. And he has given us this command:
Anyone who loves God must also love their brother and sister. —1 John 4:19, 21

MARCH 8

*D*o you see yourself the way I see you? Or are you focusing on all the things you do wrong or are not good at? Do you focus on your faults or your appearance, especially on the things you wish you could change about yourself? Tell Me, do you love yourself? I don't want this question to make you feel uneasy or guilty. I want you to be honest with Me. If your answer is anything but that you truly do love yourself, I want you to ask yourself why you feel that way? Are you believing lies that are not from Me? The truth is I love you and I want you to love yourself. I want you to let go of the lies and really love yourself. If I value you and think you are worthy enough for My Son to die for, shouldn't these thoughts be what fill your mind? My child, you are precious to Me and I dearly love you! Empty your mind of the lies and fill it up with My truths. Begin to love yourself.

For you created my inmost being; you knit me together in my mother's womb.
I praise you because I am fearfully and wonderfully made; your works are wonderful,
I know that full well. My frame was not hidden from you when I was made in the
secret place, when I was woven together in the depths of the earth.
—Psalm 139:13-15

MARCH 9

*H*ow do you interact with your spouse, family and friends? Do your moods change? Are you grouchy or stressed out? Do you take your frustrations out on those you love the most? How much fun are you to be around? Really ponder these questions. I am not trying to make you feel bad but trying to help you. I really do care about you and your loved ones. Let Me show you the better way. The Holy Spirit lives and reigns inside of you. You do not have to let your moods control you any longer. Make the choice to connect to My grace, to My ability working in you. Next time you find yourself wanting to let your emotions get the best of you, pause, let go of those thoughts, and then breathe. Connect to Me and breathe in My power, My love and My ways. Let Me fill you up to overflowing. Then you will be able to pour Me out to those you love!

Do nothing out of selfish ambition or vain conceit. Rather, in humility value others above yourselves.
—Philippians 2:3

Dear friends, let us love one another, for love comes from God. Everyone
who loves has been born of God and knows God. Dear friends, since God so
loved us, we also ought to love one another. —1 John 4:7, 11

MARCH 10

I am in your presence at all times, interacting with you. You know it in your mind, but is it really in your heart where you believe it? Look with your spiritual eyes and see what I am doing, how I interact with you. There are times I am sitting by your side watching TV with you. I join you at meals and enjoy your conversations. When you wake up at night, I am sitting right there next to you. When you're going through a difficult time, I have My arms around you. I take your hand and guide you when you don't know what to do. I sometimes kneel in front of you, gently cupping your chin and lifting up your head so that you gaze into My loving eyes. I love when you make time to spend with Me, when you are awakened and look with your spiritual eyes for where I am in the room, and how we are interacting. Become aware of My constant presence in your life. I love spending time with you.

You have searched me, Lord, and you know me. You know when I sit and when I rise;
you perceive my thoughts from afar. You discern my going out and my lying down;
you are familiar with all my ways. Before a word is on my tongue you, Lord, know it
completely. You hem me in behind and before, and you lay your hand upon me. Such
knowledge is too wonderful for me, too lofty for me to attain. —Psalm 139:1-6

$\mathcal{S}$ometimes it seems difficult to be nice to people. There can be a myriad of reasons for feeling this way, and some seem justifiable. On your own, it seems impossible to be pleasant when you don't feel like it. But you're not alone or on your own. If you truly know Me, the Holy Spirit lives in you and gives you the power to show the fruit of the spirit. You are empowered to both feel and show My love, joy, peace, patience, kindness, goodness, faithfulness, gentleness and self-control. Connect with Me and be empowered to do what you can't do on your own strength.

But the fruit of the Spirit is love, joy, peace, patience, kindness, goodness, faithfulness, gentleness, self control; against such things there is no law. Now those who belong to Christ Jesus have crucified the flesh with its passions and desires. If we live by the Spirit, let us also walk by the Spirit.
—Galatians 5:22-25 (NASB)

$\mathcal{T}$emptation is a reality and can be a struggle on a daily basis. Being tempted is not a sin, but it's what you do with that temptation that determines if it is or not. If you continue thinking about it, chances are you will act on the temptation, and that is sinful. Some temptations can be very strong and powerful, but you don't have to act on them, even if they are consuming you. I give you everything you need to resist temptation! I will not let you be tempted beyond what you can bear, for I provide a way out for you. When tempted, immediately take your focus off of it. Place your focus on Me and My strength pouring into you so you can turn your back on it. Walk away and don't look back. Stay focused on what I am doing through you. Remember I am in control, and resisting temptation can make you even stronger. I walk with you through this and am right by your side for you are never alone.

No temptation has overtaken you except what is common to mankind. And God is faithful; he will not let you be tempted beyond what you can bear. But when you are tempted, he will also provide a way out so that you can endure it.
—1 Corinthians 10:13

"Watch and pray so that you will not fall into temptation. The spirit is willing, but the flesh is weak."
—Matthew 26:41

MARCH 13

*T*here are tasks you perform that may be unpleasant, difficult, or unenjoyable. Sometimes you do them grudgingly or avoid doing them altogether. Either way, it doesn't make you feel good inside and robs you of peace. Let Me show you a better way. I want you to change how you are thinking about these tasks. Think about how I have given you strength and good health to be able to do the task. Work at it with all of your heart as if doing it for Me. Do it for My glory and in My name. Listen to praise music, sing to Me, or think of all your blessings as you perform the work. You will find by doing it this way that peace will return, and you may even find the joy in it.

And whatever you do, whether in word or deed, do it all in the name
of the Lord Jesus, giving thanks to God the Father through him.
—Colossians 3:17

Whatever you do, work at it with all your heart, as working for the Lord, not for human masters.
—Colossians 3:23

MARCH 14

*Y*ou lie in bed at night and can't fall asleep, or you wake up in the middle of the night and can't get back to sleep. What do you do during that time? Do you fret about not getting enough sleep or worry about problems, or is there anxiety? None of these come from Me. Instead, use this opportunity to spend time with Me. Picture Me sitting by you on your bed, with My comforting hand holding yours. Talk to Me and share your concerns, fears and problems, for I am the Lord of all that concerns you. Feel My peace and strength being poured into you from My hand on yours. My will for you is that when you lie down, you will not be afraid and that your sleep will be sweet.

When you lie down, you will not be afraid; when you lie down, your sleep will be sweet.
—Proverbs 3:24

In peace I will lie down and sleep, for you alone, Lord, make me dwell in safety.
—Psalm 4:8

*M*y child, I want you to trust Me completely with all your heart. In everything you do, look to Me. Do not try to figure out life from your own understanding of it; you simply can't because you are not Me. I can see the big picture from beginning to end. You can only see a small corner of the picture. Please let go of your pride and your plans and seek My face. Seek My ways according to My Word which is unchanging. It is then I will be able to guide you down the right path because you will receive My counsel, which stands the test of time.

"For my thoughts are not your thoughts, neither are your ways my ways,"
declares the Lord. As the heavens are higher than the earth, so are my ways
higher than your ways and my thoughts than your thoughts.
—Isaiah 55:8-9

For now we see only a reflection as in a mirror; then we shall see face
to face. Now I know in part; then I shall know fully, even as I am fully known.
—1 Corinthians 13:12

*L*ife has its challenges, both from a personal perspective and a world perspective. You may feel discouraged, overwhelmed or without hope as you ponder the situations. My child, please don't focus on what the world sees and their lack of solutions that would be pleasing to Me. Awaken to the reality of what I am doing in your midst that the world can not see. Even though you do not see it or any results, I am at work. The world does not report on what I am doing. Rest in knowing I am in control, and the story's end will be Mine!

Now faith is confidence in what we hope for and assurance about what we do not see.
—Hebrews 11:1

So we fix our eyes not on what is seen, but on what is unseen,
since what is seen is temporary, but what is unseen is eternal.
—2 Corinthians 4:18

I know you wonder how I can ask you in My Word to consider it pure joy whenever you face trials. That may be hard for you to understand. What could possibly be joyful about going through a crisis? Remember, My ways and thoughts are not your ways and thoughts. I want you to take your eyes off the problem and refocus on Me. Recall My nature and who I am to you. I am your rock, comforter, strength, healer, counselor, provider; I am what you need for the situation. Once you keep your mind on who I am to you, you can look for the joy. The joy is connecting to Me and being in My presence. It is in surrendering everything and allowing Me to be in control. The joy is in the testing of your faith that changes you from within to develop patience and perseverance and maturity in Me. I want to challenge you that the next time you face a trial, look for the joy and see what happens!

Consider it pure joy, my brothers and sisters, whenever you face trials of many kinds, because you know that the testing of your faith produces perseverance. Let perseverance finish its work so that you may be mature and complete, not lacking anything.
—James 1:2-4

MARCH 18

Y ou will make mistakes. You will make choices that are not pleasing to Me. You may even walk away from Me for a while. But I never walk away from you. I am always here with outstretched arms, waiting for your return, and when you come back, I am filled with joy! Let My joy become your strength as you accept My grace in your life. My grace is My ability and power working in and through you. As you trust in Me, My joy becomes your joy and gives you strength and guidance to do what is right in My eyes. I am always here to encourage you.

Nehemiah said, "Go and enjoy choice food and sweet drinks, and send some to those who have nothing prepared. This day is holy to our Lord. Do not grieve, for the joy of the Lord is your strength."
—Nehemiah 8:10

May the God of hope fill you with all joy and peace as you trust in him, so that you may overflow with hope by the power of the Holy Spirit.
—Romans 15:13

MARCH 19

*I*n the hard times, continue to persevere and seek My face. Do not dwell on any thought that is not focused on Me or My presence in your life. Instead, intentionally look for My goodness. Look for My hand in your life and recall who I am to you. Keep your eyes on Me alone. Find rest in My arms, draw in My strength and stay the course.

Blessed is the one who perseveres under trial because, having stood the test, that person will receive the crown of life that the Lord has promised to those who love him.
—James 1:12

Look to the Lord and his strength; seek his face always.
—1 Chronicles 16:11

MARCH 20

I want to bring revival into your life! I want to show you how to press into an all-consuming relationship with Me, where your thoughts are on Me constantly. It is where you will yearn to read My Word and you will start looking for ways to spend more time with Me. It is where you will come to a place where nothing matters more than your relationship with Me! When you establish this bond with Me, everything you do in life will flow out of this place and will come naturally to you because I equip you. I want to be first in your life! Ask for that desire and I will gladly give it to you.

Will you not revive us again, that your people may rejoice in you?
—Psalm 85:6

For this is what the high and exalted One says— he who lives forever, whose name is holy: I live in a high and holy place, but also with the one who is contrite and lowly in spirit, to revive the spirit of the lowly and to revive the heart of the contrite.
—Isaiah 57:15

*C*ome expectantly to Me for fresh encounters. I want you to feel My presence in a deeper way! I desire for you to experience My strength and power running through you and to feel My peace permeate all through your soul. Ask Me to bring to your mind anything that is keeping you from Me and that is getting in the way of our relationship, so you can confess it and let go of it. I am always by your side, no matter what you do or believe. I want to give you a fresh start, a fresh infusion of My love. Come, let Me be your first love!

The Lord replied, "My Presence will go with you, and I will give you rest."
—Exodus 33:14

You make known to me the path of life; you will fill me with joy in your presence, with eternal pleasures at your right hand.
—Psalm 16:11

MARCH 22

*F*rom time to time, you find yourself waiting: waiting on the phone, waiting in lines, waiting in traffic jams and waiting in countless other ways. This can be stressful, frustrating and exasperating. Let Me show you a better way to handle the waiting. Instead of focusing on the situation and the time you may feel you are wasting, refocus your thoughts on Me. Focus on My spirit living inside of you, empowering you and filling you with patience to overflowing. Let your mind stay in that place for a while. Think about the peace I am pouring into you. Meditate on that peace that the world can't understand, and when you're abiding in Me you simply will feel it and understand. You will want to stay in that place of peace once you connect to it.

We continually ask God to fill you, being strengthened with all power according to his glorious might so that you may have great endurance and patience, and giving joyful thanks to the Father, who has qualified you to share in the inheritance of his holy people in the kingdom of light.
—Colossians 1:9b, 11-12

There are times you may feel like you are wandering in the wilderness, feeling lost, discouraged, or depressed. You know in your mind all the right Scriptures, you pray and you serve Me. You want desperately for what you know and believe in your mind to travel to your heart so you can trust and experience what you know. You want so much to be at peace. My child, I want that for you also! My Son died so you can feel My peace and live in its abundance! I know you are turning to Me for answers for I know your heart. Stand fast, My child, and hold the course by persevering. Worship Me and keep your eyes fixed on Me alone. Spend time with My other children who can lift you up. Don't ever go by your feelings, for they are not a true indication of what is happening or how I am working in your life. Remember, I am right by your side, cheering you on.

Trust in the Lord with all your heart and lean not on your own understanding; in all your ways submit to him, and he will make your paths straight.
—Proverbs 3:5-6

Therefore, my dear brothers and sisters, stand firm. Let nothing move you. Always give your-selves fully to the work of the Lord, because you know that your labor in the Lord is not in vain.
—1 Corinthians 15:58

MARCH 24

Do you have something in your life that you wish would go away? It might be something irritating, draining or challenging. You don't see an end in sight, and it is wearing you down. It is the enemy's way of making you ineffective for Me and trying to steal My Word and joy from you. My Word is alive in your heart; you act on it and stand on it in faith. I want you to resist and actively fight against the enemy and see him flee. I have equipped you to do this. Simply command him to flee in My name, and he must flee. Stop focusing on the situation and focus on Me. On your own strength you are weak, but My power is in you. My joy and peace are yours even in the situation that may not go away. Know the truth and be set free!

Therefore, in order to keep me from becoming conceited, I was given a thorn in my flesh, a messen-ger of Satan, to torment me. Three times I pleaded with the Lord to take it away from me. But he said to me, "My grace is sufficient for you, for my power is made perfect in weakness." Therefore I will boast all the more gladly about my weaknesses, so that Christ's power may rest on me.
—2 Corinthians 12:7a-9

$\mathcal{T}$here are times you wonder why I'm not addressing your concerns and answering your prayers fast enough. You wonder if I am hearing you and if I even care. My child, I do hear you, and I know everything about your concerns. I do care deeply and I want the best for you. In your eyes you think you are waiting longer than you like, but in My eyes I am preparing you and growing your character so you can better handle life's challenges in the future. In this waiting time, renew your mind. Stop focusing on the situation and lack of closure, and refocus on things that will help give you patience and peace and grow your character. Think on the truths you know: that I am sovereign, in control, and am right by your side; that you have access to My patience, peace and strength. Think about Biblical stories that demonstrate this, like the story of Joseph and all the waiting and preparation he went through until his prayers were answered. At My perfect timing, you will see what I see!

When Joseph's brothers saw that their father was dead, they said, "What if Joseph holds a grudge against us and pays us back for all the wrongs we did to him?" But Joseph said to them, "Don't be afraid. Am I in the place of God? You intended to harm me, but God intended it for good to accomplish what is now being done, the saving of many lives.
—Genesis 50:15, 19-20

MARCH 26

$\mathcal{S}$ometimes you wonder where I am. You are going through challenges and don't see Me anywhere. Your faith may waiver and you may even begin to question. It is during these times that I want you to begin to look for encouragement and answers in My Word. Look at what I did for Daniel and draw faith from this true story. Even though I was unseen to Daniel, I was there protecting him from the mouth of the lion. Daniel knew and trusted Me and put his faith in Me. His eyes weren't on the lion but on Me. Won't you do the same?

Daniel answered, "May the king live forever! My God sent his angel, and he shut the mouths of the lions. They have not hurt me, because I was found innocent in his sight. Nor have I ever done any wrong before you, Your Majesty."
—Daniel 6:21-22

$\mathcal{M}$y desire for you is that you begin to hunger for more of Me and My glory. It doesn't matter where you are in your walk with Me, there is always more for you to learn, to receive and become awakened to. I want you to desire to have My heart for people and to see them as I see them. I want you to know Me more intimately and better understand My nature and character. I desire for you to have My mind so you can begin to grasp how I think, better understand My ways and love people like I do. I want you to understand and apply My Word in your life. I want to show you how to see the unseen and what I am doing and to hear more clearly when I speak to you. I want you to surrender your life to Me and to awaken to all the possibilities of everything I want to give you. It will change your life!

For this reason, since the day we heard about you, we have not stopped praying for you. We continually ask God to fill you with the knowledge of his will through all the wisdom and understanding that the Spirit gives, so that you may live a life worthy of the Lord and please him in every way: bearing fruit in every good work, growing in the knowledge of God.
—Colossians 1:9-10

$\mathcal{A}$re you aware, My child, that I am constantly interacting with you? Think of Me as a pipeline constantly pouring out encouragement, empowerment and guidance for each day. When you are tired, I fill you with strength, stamina and mental alertness. When you are stressed, I pour out My calm and peace. When you are drained, I fill you up so that you are refreshed and recharged. Depending on what situation you are in, My pipeline fills you with discernment, healing, grace and provision to bring about the fruit of the spirit. No matter what you face, I am giving you what you need. Look for it and depend on it. It is there pouring into you right now!

And to know this love that surpasses knowledge—that you may be filled to the measure of all the fullness of God.
—Ephesians 3:19

Nevertheless, as surely as I live and as surely as the glory of the Lord fills the whole earth.
—Numbers 14:21

The cross can change your life! When you understand the finished work of the cross, it gives you access to the abundant life found in Me. Because of the cross, you are free to come into My presence and interact with Me any time you want. Worries, sickness, sin, fear and anything else you struggle with have been conquered at the cross, and none of these things have control over you any longer unless you allow them to. You are free to let go of everything you are dealing with and to keep your eyes and thoughts fully focused on Me. You begin to realize that I am in control of your life and want My best for you. You are now able to feel My comfort strengthening and uplifting you. Because of the cross, you have access to My peace which is a peace that man can't understand. No matter what you are facing, you can rest in My peaceful state. My Son laid down His life for you to set you free because I love you that much! Come, partake of this abundant life that the cross has given you.

For the message of the cross is foolishness to those who are perishing, but to us who are being saved it is the power of God.
—1 Corinthians 1:18

The thief comes only to steal and kill and destroy; I came that they may have life, and have it abundantly. —John 10:10 (NASB)

I care about your character, who you truly are inside. I value integrity and want you to value it, too. Every day you have opportunities to demonstrate honesty and strong moral principles and to do what is pleasing to Me. Even when the temptation is great, you are empowered to do what is right in My sight and not to succumb to that desire. Remember, you have a new nature in Me! I encourage you to partake of My divine nature that is in you and walk in My ways in all that you do.

For we are taking pains to do what is right, not only in the eyes of the Lord but also in the eyes of man.
—2 Corinthians 8:21

Whoever walks in integrity walks securely, but whoever takes crooked paths will be found out.
—Proverbs 10:9

*Y*ou find yourself in an unexpected situation that is turning into a huge life storm. You weren't prepared for it and you find yourself at a complete loss. Fear paralyzes you and you think you can't go on. You can't think straight and can't see a quick fix or solution. You want to give up in anguish and despair. My child, turn to Me; cry out to Me. You don't even need words; your heart will say it all. I will give you hope. I will guide you and give you direction. I will give you eyes to see what I see and what I am doing. Ask Me to guard your heart, mind and health, and I will. Take every negative and fearful thought captive and make it obedient to Christ. Stay constantly connected to Me by recalling My promises, reading My Word and spending time in My presence. Praise Me and find things in your life to be thankful for. Get to know My nature and who I am to you. Fear does not have to paralyze you if you renounce it in Jesus' name. And remember, you will get through this storm with Me by your side or with Me carrying you all the way.

We demolish arguments and every pretension that sets itself up against the knowledge of God, and we take captive every thought to make it obedient to Christ.
—2 Corinthians 10:5

Trust in the Lord with all your heart and lean not on your own understanding; in all your ways submit to him, and he will make your paths straight.
—Proverbs 3:5-6

APRIL 1

*T*ake time to remember the events of the last supper, which was the final meal My Son shared with His disciples before His arrest and crucifixion. Even though He already knew the events that would take place, He showed grace to all the disciples who betrayed and deserted Him. Reflect on the cup that was poured out for you, which was His blood shed for you. This is the new covenant in His blood. Through this act you have direct access to Me, your Heavenly Father. Reflect on the bread that represents His body, which was given for you to conquer sin, death and all the worries and hardships you carry. Remember My Son and how He taught the disciples the principle of servanthood as He washed their feet. Remember what His death means to you, the atonement for your sins and all mankind's. Reflect on My Son's perfect sacrifice, and through your faith in receiving Him, you will live with Me forever!

After taking the cup, he gave thanks and said, "Take this and divide it among you.
For I tell you I will not drink again from the fruit of the vine until the kingdom of God comes."
And he took bread, gave thanks and broke it, and gave it to them, saying, "This is my body
given for you; do this in remembrance of me." In the same way, after the supper he took the
cup, saying, "This cup is the new covenant in my blood, which is poured out for you."
—Luke 22:17-20

APRIL 2

*W*hile nailed to the cross, My Son's thoughts were about His love and sorrow over mankind. But specifically, His thoughts were about you, for He loved you that much. He proved to you on that day the great length He would go to display this love. Take time to remember and reflect on what He endured. What I want you to learn from this is to lay down everything at the foot of the cross including your very life, your burdens, trials and sin. It is finished. Jesus has taken care of it all! These things do not have to weigh you down or affect your life any longer. I also want you to reflect on My love for you and all of mankind. I give you this same capacity to love others as I love. Go in My name and do likewise. Share about what My Son did for them also.

This is how we know what love is: Jesus Christ laid down his life for us.
And we ought to lay down our lives for our brothers and sisters.
—1 John 3:16

But he was pierced for our transgressions, he was crushed for our iniquities;
the punishment that brought us peace was on him, and by his wounds we are healed.
—Isaiah 53:5

APRIL 3

*Y*our life starts at the cross. My Son died to take sin, baggage, bondage and everything that hinders you out of your life, to wipe it clean and give you a new transformed life and a new beginning. Proclaim its power. Jesus thought of you while hanging on the cross. He did it for you because He loved you that much. Because of the cross, I see you as righteous. Proclaim it, declare it and walk in your new identity. You are not an orphan but My child with all the rights and benefits of being My heir. With them you have My power to conquer anything you struggle with. You are more than a conqueror because I give that power to you as My child. The cross gives you victory. It gives you encouragement and hope. You find rest in the cross. Nothing you struggle with is too big. I want you to look at the cross with new eyes.

For the message of the cross is foolishness to those who are perishing
but to us who are being saved it is the power of God.
—1 Corinthians 1:18

"He himself bore our sins" in his body on the cross, so that we might die to sins and live for righteousness; "by his wounds you have been healed." For "you were like sheep going astray," but now you have returned to the Shepherd and Overseer of your souls.
—1 Peter 2:24-25

APRIL 4

*M*y dear child, I love when you worship Me and when you sing right to Me as if I'm there in front of you. I am there you know, for I am constantly with you. When you take time to worship and spend time with Me each day, it warms My heart, and I take great delight in it. You have no idea how much I want to lavish My love on you simply because you are My child and I am your Father. I offer you more than your earthly Father ever could, for I am the perfect Father. My plan for your future has always been filled with hope because I love you with an everlasting love. I will never stop doing good things for you. I want to show you great and marvelous things. If you seek Me with all your heart, you will find Me. Will you do that, My child? Will you trust Me? I love you more than you will ever know. Please receive that love.

Stand up and praise the Lord your God, who is from everlasting to everlasting. Blessed be your glorious name, and may it be exalted above all blessing and praise. You alone are the Lord. You made the heavens, even the highest heavens, and all their starry host, the earth and all that is on it, the seas and all that is in them. You give life to everything, and the multitudes of heaven worship you.
—Nehemiah 9:5b-6

*D*o you know what I think about you? You are absolutely amazing! I created you in My image and you were definitely worth dying for. Can you comprehend how remarkable you are and how much I value you? I don't see the sin; all I see in you is My Son, who washed away that sin with His blood. I look at you and what I see is My splendor and all My glory and power in you, just waiting for you to recognize it's there. Once you see it then you can use it to radiate My love to others. Let that sink in and write it on your heart. This IS who you are!

Keep me as the apple of your eye; hide me in the shadow of your wings.

—Psalm 17:8

God made him who had no sin to be sin for us, so that in him we might become the righteousness of God.

—2 Corinthians 5:21

*M*y child, I am burning with desire for you to come to your Heavenly Father and to know Me as your Daddy. Come and spend time with Me. Tell Me your desires and hopes and plans. Yes, I do know them already and I also know everything about your future, but I desire that time together. Tell Me your concerns and what troubles your heart so I can bring you comfort and direction. Let Me join you when you read a book, watch TV, or work on your laptop. Pause for a moment throughout the day to stay connected to Me. I am really right there next to you, and it delights Me when you realize that. I really do care and love you so much!

Before they call I will answer; while they are still speaking I will hear.

—Isaiah 65:24

The Lord appeared to us in the past, saying: "I have loved you with an everlasting love; I have drawn you with unfailing kindness."

—Jeremiah 31:3

*N*othing in your life matters more than knowing Me. It is the most important thing you can do. Nothing you say or do on your own can compare with this. Set your goal on pursuing and knowing Me completely. I want you to understand My ways and My nature so that you will be found in Me and operate your life out of your relationship with Me. Your righteousness does not come from things you do, but comes only through Me and from faith in Me. Please pursue Me with all of your heart, for that is My desire for you.

But whatever were gains to me I now consider loss for the sake of Christ.
What is more, I consider everything a loss because of the surpassing worth
of knowing Christ Jesus my Lord, for whose sake I have lost all things.
I consider them garbage, that I may gain Christ and be found in him.
—Philippians 3:7-9a

*E*verywhere you turn there is injustice. It is all over this nation and getting worse. Every day there are new reports. You think to yourself, "What can I do?" You feel so helpless. Anger wells up inside of you, followed by bitterness. It can consume you. Please don't let it consume you. Make a conscious decision to let it go. I ask that you be at peace, in spite of the injustice. Vengeance is Mine and I will repay. I will judge My people. The most important thing you can do is continue to pray for this nation and its people. Your jobs are also to forgive, show compassion and then let go.

For we know him who said, "It is mine to avenge; I will
repay,"and again, "The Lord will judge his people."
—Hebrews 10:30

If my people, who are called by my name, will humble themselves and pray
and seek my face and turn from their wicked ways, then I will hear from heaven,
and I will forgive their sin and will heal their land.
—2 Chronicles 7:14

*S*o often when things are going well, you feel good about yourself and life. But the moment hardships come that you can't change, the good feelings vanish. It breaks My heart when I see you like that. I want you to learn and practice the secret of being content, just like Paul learned with all the difficulties he faced. Being content means you accept things just as they are and realize you have My power in you to penetrate into your weaknesses so you can adapt to circumstances that are not to your liking. It means being able to accept by faith and rely on Me to give you everything you need for the situation you face. When you try to control events and fight against the situation, it just leads to frustration and stress over what you can't change. Instead, trust Me to work out My perfect plan for you, to change you from the inside by working on your heart. It is then that you will experience the joy of trusting in Me and experience contentment.

I have learned to be content whatever the circumstances. I know what it is to be in need, and I know what it is to have plenty. I have learned the secret of being content in any and every situation, whether well fed or hungry, whether living in plenty or in want. I can do all this through Him who gives me strength.
—Philippians 4:11b-13

*W*hen you do something that is displeasing to Me, I want you to repent. When you repent, it is a choice to consciously turn away from what is displeasing to Me. Repenting is also making a conscious decision to change how you think. In order to do that, you must be willing to surrender completely all of your thoughts, views and opinions. It is then that your heart will allow Me to give you My thoughts, views and opinions. You will find this process will give you peace. It is a better way!

Repent, then, and turn to God, so that your sins may be wiped out that times of refreshing may come from the Lord.
—Acts 3:19

I have declared to both Jews and Greeks that they must turn to God in repentance and have faith in our Lord Jesus.
—Acts 20:21

APRIL 11

Give Me your worship and connect to Me. When you are connected to Me, it is like a pipeline that continually fills you with My peace, strength, comfort and even My joy! This will supersede anything you are facing because My spirit and power are that strong. When you are connected, you continually hear My voice speaking words of encouragement and guidance to you. You are able to see what I am doing as I model and demonstrate how to follow suit. I empower you with gifts from the Holy Spirit to bring life to others, which in turn gives you joy. This makes a big difference in My kingdom!

Show me your ways, Lord, teach me your paths. Guide me in your truth and teach me, for you are God my Savior, and my hope is in you all day long.
—Psalm 25:4-5

And I will ask the Father, and he will give you another advocate to help you and be with you forever—the Spirit of truth. The world cannot accept him, because it neither sees him nor knows him. But you know him, for he lives with you and will be in you.
—John 14:16-17

APRIL 12

You get so caught up in your problems that your goal is to find solutions on your own. Your focus is on what you can do to fix the situation. You ask others, you fret and ponder what to do, but nothing is changed. You completely forget that I am here. It is only after you exhaust all avenues that your thoughts turn to Me. It is then you ask for My help. There is no condemnation in this, but let Me show you a better way because I care about you. Allow Me to be whom you come to first. Tell Me what the problem is and allow Me to help you. Let Me be your first option, not your last ditch effort.

Ask and it will be given to you; seek and you will find; knock and the door will be opened to you.
—Matthew 7:7

Call on me in the day of trouble; I will deliver you, and you will honor me.
—Psalm 50:15

APRIL 13

I have empowered you to fight the good fight. Even when life's problems get you down, I want you to focus on finishing the race and keeping the faith. I am cheering you on! I know it may seem really hard sometimes, but remember that My strength, which I give you, is sufficient for all of your needs. My glory is displayed when you are weak. Embrace My strength and power being poured into you. There is a prize at the end of the race, which is a crown of righteousness! Keep your focus on Me and the finish line.

I have fought the good fight, I have finished the race, I have kept the faith. Now there is in store for me the crown of righteousness, which the Lord, the righteous Judge, will award to me on that day—and not only to me, but also to all who have longed for his appearing.
—2 Timothy 4:7-8

APRIL 14

I want you to become aware of My presence. I'm sitting with you when you are in the car and when you watch TV. I watch you as you sleep and I am always by your side. I know everything you think about and all that you do. It's important to Me that you know how much I love you. These are not empty words, My child, but come straight from My heart! As I lovingly formed you in your mother's womb, I thought about the wonderful plans I had for you. These plans are to prosper you and never to harm you. These plans I have for you are to give you hope for your future. I want your future to be wonderful and full of joy! That doesn't mean there won't be problems in your life. There will be, but I am always guiding you and walking by your side. I even hold you in My loving arms when things seem so hard. It is in these difficult times I am holding you very close, whispering to you, "It will be okay; I am here." You can trust Me. I will walk with you always.

This is love: not that we loved God, but that he loved us and sent his Son as an atoning sacrifice for our sins.
—1 John 4:10

God did this so that they would seek him and perhaps reach out for him and find him, though he is not far from any one of us. 'For in him we live and move and have our being.' As some of your own poets have said, 'We are his offspring.'
—Acts 17:27-28

$\mathcal{S}$ome things in life are hard to understand and comprehend. You can't see everything with your eyes, but you still believe. You cannot see wind, but you see the leaves blow in the trees and you know it is the wind that is making them move. You cannot see everything that I have promised you, but when you know Me and who I am, you can be certain My promises will come to pass. Get to know Me better through learning about My nature and character. Recall My promises and hold them close to your heart. Faith is being sure of what you hope for and certain of what you do not see. It is a sign of maturity when you have this faith. Press in to this maturity. I will gladly help you!

Now faith is confidence in what we hope for and assurance about what we do not see. And without faith it is impossible to please God, because anyone who comes to him must believe that he exists and that he rewards those who earnestly seek him.
—Hebrews 11:1, 6

For no word from God will ever fail.
—Luke 1:37

$\mathcal{T}$here are times I desire for you to quiet your mind and heart and just be still before Me. It is in these times I don't want you to pray for anything or even worship or praise Me. I don't want you to do anything except come into My presence and just BE. I know it is difficult to do. You're used to praying and worshiping Me, and I love when you do that, but I desire this from you too. Intentionally turn off your thoughts and distractions that you are constantly aware of. Then, draw closer to Me. Come into My presence. Seek it with all of your heart. Bask in My glory falling on you. You may not "feel" anything, but don't let that be a concern. There is something happening. Press in for your heart to touch My heart and your spirit to meet Mine. Wait longingly for Me, and sense My moving within you. It is in this stillness that you come into a deeper relationship with Me that will change you and, in turn, will give Me great delight!

Truly my soul finds rest in God; my salvation comes from him. Truly he is my rock and my salvation; he is my fortress, I will never be shaken. Yes, my soul, find rest in God; my hope comes from him.
—Psalm 62:1-2, 5

*H*ow many times do you think about what you don't have and focus and dwell on that? You notice it doesn't make you feel very good. I know that isn't your intention and that you truly are thankful for what you have, yet you gravitate back to those thoughts of what you lack. Let Me help you with this. Ask Me to help you become aware of when your thoughts go down this path. I will give you the self-control to stop the thought as soon as you are aware of it. Then purposefully choose to thank Me for what you have. Think about the things you take for granted; if you didn't have them any more, you would miss them. Become thankful for these things. Make it a habit to start focusing on all that you are thankful for and see the difference it will make.

Give thanks to the Lord, for he is good; his love endures forever. —Psalm 107:1

Always give thanks to God the Father for everything, in the name of our Lord Jesus Christ.
—Ephesians 5:20

APRIL 18

I notice you are holding back from Me. You are keeping part of your heart away from Me. Are you even aware that you are? I ask this in a loving way because I want the best for you! Even though you are doing this, I still am by your side, desiring all of your heart and waiting patiently. Do you know why you are doing this? Whatever the reason, it is a lie and not from Me. I want all of you which is your love, trust and confidence in Me. I won't let you down. My Word is full of My promises that are all there for you. Open up your heart fully and let Me in. Let Me continue to reside in your heart.

My son, give me your heart and let your eyes delight in my ways. —Proverbs 23:26

Create in me a pure heart, O God, and renew a steadfast spirit within me.
—Psalm 51:10

APRIL 19

*W*hen you are in distress, call on My name. I am near to you even before you cry out to Me. I will answer your cries for help. Even when you feel as if you are almost swallowed up in the depth of the crisis or perceive that there is no way out, I will rescue you and bring you up out of the pit. I give you strength, focus and patience to endure and to persevere. All the while I undergird you with a foundation that won't waiver. You can count on Me and I will answer. You are not alone!

The Lord is near to all who call on him, to all who call on him in truth.
He fulfills the desires of those who fear him; he hears their cry and saves them.
—Psalm 145:18-19

He said: "In my distress I called to the Lord, and he answered me.
From deep in the realm of the dead I called for help, and you listened to my cry."
—Jonah 2:2

APRIL 20

*M*y dear child, do you want to feel contentment, peace and joy no matter what you are going through? Then diligently and intentionally seek My presence. Learn to make it your very first priority. Seek Me with your mind and your whole heart. Don't let anything else get in the way, not even the trials you are facing. Focus on Me, not the trials. You will find My presence as you worship Me, focusing on My nature and My promises to you. You will find Me as you sing praise songs and hymns to Me or start sharing with Me all the things you are thankful for. Even in the stillness when you quiet your heart, I will be found. All these things keep your focus and attention on Me and will give you peace.

And the God of all grace, who called you to his eternal glory in Christ, after you have
suffered a little while, will himself restore you and make you strong, firm and steadfast.
—1 Peter 5:10

The Lord will fight for you; you need only to be still.
—Exodus 14:14

APRIL 21

*L*et Me give you fresh insight into how to view this world and your situations. Look at it through My eyes instead of your own. I do not worry or fear for you because I know I am Lord of your life, and everything I do for you is good, pleasing and perfect. I want you to see it that way, too. I know it may be hard at first to let go of control, but I encourage you to do this. When you truly know Me and My nature, it becomes much easier. I want you to rest in Me as you go about your daily life. I am always by your side interacting with you and pouring My life into you. When things aren't going well in your life, I am there to give you peace, strength and hope. I fill you with joy as you keep your focus on Me and who I am to you. Grow into this abundant life I sacrificed My Son for and that I so desperately want you to have.

Therefore I tell you, do not worry about your life, what you will eat or drink; or about your body, what you will wear. Is not life more than food, and the body more than clothes? Look at the birds of the air; they do not sow or reap or store away in barns, and yet your heavenly Father feeds them. Are you not much more valuable than they? Can any one of you by worrying add a single hour to your life?
—Matthew 6:25-27

APRIL 22

*M*y dearly loved child, I desire for you to know who I am to you so that you live your life out of this knowledge. I am watching over you every minute, giving you strength when you run out and guiding you when you have decisions to make and you're just unsure. I am sustaining you when you don't know how to keep on going and steering you away from danger and temptations. I daily recharge and refresh you. Most of all, I give you hope for what lies ahead. May this bring comfort to you and encourage you for each new day.

As for God, his way is perfect: The Lord's word is flawless; he shields all who take refuge in him.
—Psalm 18:30

Every good and perfect gift is from above, coming down from the Father of the heavenly lights, who does not change like shifting shadows.
—James 1:17

$\mathcal{D}$o you know what would give Me joy today? For you to take a few moments and come into My presence. Think of Me as your Abba Father, your Daddy, for that is one of the ways I present Myself to you. I am your loving Daddy, waiting for you. Picture yourself excitedly running towards Me as a little child would do, running straight into My loving arms that are outstretched, ready to pick you up, hold you and twirl you around. As you picture us meeting in this way, visualize Me throwing My head back with laughter, for I am so delighted by your coming and wanting to spend time with Me! That really is what I am doing when you come into My presence. That gives Me such great delight. It is important to Me that you know this.

Come near to God and he will come near to you.

—James 4:8a

The Spirit you received does not make you slaves, so that you live in fear again; rather, the Spirit you received brought about your adoption to sonship. And by him we cry, "Abba, Father."
—Romans 8:15

$\mathcal{E}$verything you do is in preparation for what is to come. I want you to expand your thinking and expand your horizons. Be stretched and open your mind up to new possibilities. Remember you have My boldness and My confidence because My spirit resides in you. Look for what you couldn't do in your own strength. Now that you know I equip and empower you, intentionally look for those things you can do in My strength! See what I see and do what you see Me doing.

Jesus gave them this answer: "Very truly I tell you, the Son can do nothing by himself; he can do only what he sees his Father doing, because whatever the Father does the Son also does. For the Father loves the Son and shows him all he does. Yes, and he will show him even greater works than these, so that you will be amazed.
—John 5:19-20

So Jesus said, "When you have lifted up the Son of Man, then you will know that I am he and that I do nothing on my own but speak just what the Father has taught me.
—John 8:28

APRIL 25

*A*s you worship or sing songs directly to Me, you come into My presence. It's as simple as that. When you allow your mind to be free of everything that clutters and hinders and allow your heart to be open to everything I want you to experience, you step into My presence! Sometimes it's just a quiet peace that flows over you, sometimes you may hear Me whisper to you through a thought, or sometimes you may actually experience My nearness. My presence is experienced in different ways and they are all good. As you learn to go deeper, seeking more, you may even feel a connection— spirit to spirit, heart to heart. It may even bring tears to your eyes, it is that wonderful. Come, draw near to Me. Come even closer, leaving all the things of this world behind to feel My loving arms around you. Feel My love pour into you and My peace flow through you. Experience total contentment. Walk into My joy that can fill you to overflowing. All these things I want to give you no matter what is going on in your life. Will you give Me your heart and allow My glory to fill you to overflowing? It will change your life and will set you free.

But as for me, it is good to be near God. I have made the Sovereign Lord my refuge; I will tell of all your deeds. —Psalm 73:28

APRIL 26

*S*tand firm on My truths and My promises to you found in My Word. Memorize them and recall them when you need encouragement, strength, or perseverance. Do not waiver or second guess anything. That is just the enemy trying to influence you. Be bold in My boldness. Speak My truth to others to give them encouragement. Speak My truth to give correction, remembering to do so with My love. My Word is like a solid rock that will not be moved or changed.

Then you will know the truth, and the truth will set you free. —John 8:32

The grass withers and the flowers fall, but the word of our God endures forever. —Isaiah 40:8

*C*ome stand before Me in worship with your heart wide open, holding nothing back, so that you can receive all I want to give you. You have only tasted a very small portion of My endless bounty, and what you have tasted has been good and leaves you wanting more. Loosen your grip and let go of all control and pride. That is of utmost importance! Let Me fill you with My living water. My floodgates are open to you. Let the refreshing waters flow over you. Watch as the healing waters rise up over your body. Don't fear as the water rises above your head and covers it. It is at this time you must trust in My nature. It is covering your entire body for a reason. Rest in My presence as you are totally submerged. Remember, there is nothing to fear; I am in control. As the waters recede, you are transformed. You gave Me everything and experienced what that is like, laying everything down and trusting Me totally. Recall this moment daily, how I demonstrated for you that I am everything you need.

When you pass through the waters, I will be with you; and when you pass through the rivers, they will not sweep over you. When you walk through the fire, you will not be burned; the flames will not set you ablaze.

—Isaiah 43:2

---

*A*s you go about your day, especially when you are stressed or your day isn't going as planned and you feel overwhelmed, take a moment to empty your mind and then breathe. Breathe Me in. Breathe in My life that is pouring into you. Breathe in all My goodness. Reflect on this. Linger here… and repeat often! Sometimes a moment with Me is all you need.

I will refresh the weary and satisfy the faint.

—Jeremiah 31:25

For God alone, O my soul, wait in silence, for my hope is from him.

—Psalm 62:5 (ESV)

APRIL 29

There are times you get discouraged as you perceive nothing is changing in your circumstances or you don't see a way out of a situation. You feel that life is passing you by, or you are just trying to get through another day. You feel you are seeking Me and following My ways, but yet you are discouraged and may think, "What is the use?" for you don't see anything happening. My child, don't give up, for I am right there with you! I am so pleased you are persevering, even though you don't see results. None of it is in vain. Remember, don't look at things through your eyes. Focus on seeing things the way I see them. Ask for My help in learning to see what I see. Know that I am at work in your life and be encouraged.

Not only so, but we also glory in our sufferings, because we know that suffering produces perseverance; perseverance, character; and character, hope. And hope does not put us to shame, because God's love has been poured out into our hearts through the Holy Spirit, who has been given to us.
—Romans 5:3-5

Therefore, my dear brothers and sisters, stand firm. Let nothing move you. Always give your- selves fully to the work of the Lord, because you know that your labor in the Lord is not in vain.
—1 Corinthians 15:58

APRIL 30

My child, do not walk in fear. Do not focus on what you are facing or the emo- tions that try to overtake you. You are My child and I have your back! I walk with you through the powerful storm. I carry you over the high raging waters. I shield you from the flames that destroy. When you get news that is discouraging or frightening, please turn to Me and keep your focus here. Find Me in the situation and in the storm you face. For I am there, guiding you through it.

Then he got into the boat and his disciples followed him. Suddenly a furious storm came up on the lake, so that the waves swept over the boat. But Jesus was sleeping. The disciples went and woke him, saying, "Lord, save us! We're going to drown!" He replied, "You of little faith, why are you so afraid?" Then he got up and rebuked the winds and the waves, and it was completely calm. The men were amazed and asked, "What kind of man is this? Even the winds and the waves obey him!"
—Matthew 8:23-27

MAY 1

I see you worrying, My child. I see your anxious thoughts every day. You try not to worry, but your thoughts go back to that place without realizing it. Other times it is an overwhelming feeling that you struggle with minute by minute. Why do you worry, My dear one? Do you think that it will change the outcome somehow or that subconsciously worrying is necessary for the situation to work out? Does it really make you feel better to worry? Let Me show you the better way. I want you to give Me all your worries and then leave them with Me. Don't keep taking them back, like you don't believe I can help you. I know you don't feel that way on the surface, but deep down if you're honest with yourself, you doubt. I really do care and want the best for you. I have the strength and desire to carry all of your burdens. In return I give you peace when you are fearful, strength when you are weak, rest for your soul and wisdom and guidance when you don't know what to do. Most of all I wipe away every tear from your face and carry you through the situation until it is over. This is who I am, for this is My nature! Let go and believe!

So do not fear, for I am with you; do not be dismayed, for I am your God.
I will strengthen you and help you; I will uphold you with my righteous right hand.
—Isaiah 41:10

MAY 2

I want to give you encouragement as you face a situation you have no control over or don't know what to do about it. I have already arranged a plan for you beyond what you can imagine or dream up. No one has ever heard it or seen it, for it is that special and unique. Awaken yourself to what I have for you, to what I am doing that you aren't even aware of. Be open to the possibilities. I give good gifts to My children who love Me.

But, as it is written, "What no eye has seen, nor ear heard,
nor the heart of man imagined, what God has prepared for those who love him."
—1 Corinthians 2:9 (ESV)

MAY 3

$\mathcal{D}$o you know that I pour out My blessings on your life each day? My heart is to bless you and watch over you night and day. I want you to become aware of this fact because it will be a comfort to you. I bless you and keep you and My face shines upon you. I pour out My grace on you and give you My peace that man can not offer. I watch over you with a perfect Father's protective love. Become aware of My nearness to you and all these blessings I give you. Soak in it by meditating on these words. Repeat often.

The Lord bless you and keep you; the Lord make his face shine on you
and be gracious to you; the Lord turn his face toward you and give you peace.
—Numbers 6:24-26

MAY 4

$\mathcal{I}$ am the Great Heart Surgeon. I have been working on your heart. Have you noticed how I have lovingly brought to your attention things that aren't pleasing to Me in what you think, say and do? And when you noticed these things that I have helped you become aware of, how I would then show you the better way? I want to give you a new heart! Exchange a heart that is world-centered for a heart that is centered on Me. I've already been doing the work and preparing the foundation. Do you want this new heart for the things that I have a heart for? If you really, truly desire this heart, it is yours!

I will give them an undivided heart and put a new spirit in them;
I will remove from them their heart of stone and give them a heart of flesh.
—Ezekiel 11:19

Come near to God and he will come near to you. Wash your hands
you sinners, and purify your hearts, you double-minded.
—James 4:8

MAY 5

*A*re you aware that there is more I want to give you? More that you already possess as My child but aren't aware of? I want to awaken you to this idea that there is so much more. Do you ever ask Me for more? Begin to hunger for it. I want you to experience My presence in ways you haven't experienced so far. I want to give you My heart, My compassion for all people. I want you to think how I think. I want you to see situations the way I see them. I want you to do what you see Me doing— healing and ministering to people with the power and authority you already have as a believer. I want you to seek and operate in the spiritual gift or gifts I have given you. Are you aware of this gift or gifts you already have? Would you pursue finding out what it is and begin to use it? You will be blessed if you do. All these things I want you to experience will add a new and welcome dimension to your life. There is even more than these things I have mentioned. Awaken to the 'more', ask for it, pursue it and watch how your life will be enhanced and changed in a wonderful way!

Look to the Lord and his strength; seek his face always.
—1 Chronicles 16:11

The lions may grow weak and hungry, but those who seek the Lord lack no good thing.
—Psalm 34:10

MAY 6

*W*hen you feel discouraged, know that is not from Me. That comes solely from the enemy whose goal is to kill, steal and destroy. Please don't succumb to his tactics or be dismayed. Please don't dwell on what you are feeling, but turn your focus to Me. I hear your cries and your distress, for I am near to the brokenhearted. I am your God and you have My strength pouring into you! This is My promise to you. Look for what I am doing in you and be encouraged!

What, then, shall we say in response to these things? If God is for us, who can be against us?
—Romans 8:31

"I have told you these things, so that in me you may have peace.
In this world you will have trouble. But take heart! I have overcome the world."
—John 16:33

*W*here is your rest? I ask that not in a condemning way but out of My loving concern for you. I see that you are sometimes so weary from life in general and the burdens you choose to carry that are weighing you down. Some days it is an effort for you to just get through the day. My heart goes out to you and I grieve watching you like this. My child, it doesn't have to be this way. Don't believe the lies that say, "This is how it has to be and nothing will ever change" or "I can do this on my own". Turn your back on your pride. Ask Me if there is anything else you need to let go of that prevents you from following My ways. I want you to come to Me. That is a command and requires an action on your part. It takes trust in knowing who I am. I give a promise to you that I will give you rest for it is attainable, but, My child, it has to be My way which will not fail. Please take My yoke upon you and learn from Me. This again takes an action on your part in trusting Me. It takes letting go of wanting to be in control and surrendering that control to Me, the Father that loves you and wants the best for you! After you purposefully take My yoke, I ask you to learn from Me, which means you have to know Me and also see what I am doing. It may take time getting to know My ways, but it is worth the effort. Spend time with Me and ask Me to show you these ways. I am waiting with open arms to help guide you. You will then see just how gentle and humble in heart I really am! This will bring you into greater intimacy with Me which will delight Me greatly! By following My ways, you will find the rest for your soul that you seek. It is a wonderful place to be and a great place to linger. That is My great desire, to see you remain in this place. By yielding to My way of reaching this place of rest, you will see that My yoke is easy and My burden is light. After the initial letting go of control, My ways are really quite simple and easy to attain because I am doing the work in you. Won't you come to Me and find rest?

"Come to me, all you who are weary and burdened, and I will give you rest.
Take my yoke upon you and learn from me, for I am gentle and humble in heart,
and you will find rest for your souls. For my yoke is easy and my burden is light."
—Matthew 11:28-30

MAY 8

*T*he world sees the enemy as very powerful, but in My sight he is powerless! Stop looking at what the world says and sees. I want you to see what I see. Hold on to the fact that he has been defeated by My Son, once and for all times. You have My power flowing through you since you are My child. It is the same power that raised Jesus from the dead! Think of it. That is amazing power, and you, My child, are a carrier of that power! I have given you authority in Jesus' name to command the enemy to flee! Use that power and authority. It is your gift as My heir!

*I have given you authority to trample on snakes and scorpions
and to overcome all the power of the enemy; nothing will harm you.*

—Luke 10:19

*I will give you the keys of the kingdom of heaven; whatever you bind on earth
will be bound in heaven, and whatever you loose on earth will be loosed in heaven.*

—Matthew 16:19

MAY 9

I see your frustration, My child. You continue to do what you don't want to do and don't do what you really want to do which is what would be pleasing to Me. You agonize over this and hate that you are this way. Condemning yourself isn't the answer, though. Stop and refocus your thoughts. You can't do what is pleasing to Me by your own strength. But you have been made new, for My spirit lives in you! Keep your mind on this truth. You may still stumble, but as soon as you realize it, just refocus without blaming yourself. Step into My power working in you! Then you will do what is pleasing in My sight.

*I do not understand what I do. For what I want to do I do not do, but what I hate I do.
Although I want to do good, evil is right there with me. For in my inner being I delight
in God's law; but I see another law at work in me, waging war against the law of my
mind and making me a prisoner of the law of sin at work within me. What a wretched
man I am! Who will rescue me from this body that is subject to death? Thanks be to
God, who delivers me through Jesus Christ our Lord!*

—Romans 7:15, 21b-25a

*M*y child, I am always with you! No matter what you are doing during the day or night, I never leave your side. I know everything about you, all that you think about and all that you do. Nothing is hidden from My sight. I want you to know just how much I love you. These are not words to take lightly. They are spoken from My heart to yours. Who do you listen to? Are you listening to the lies of the enemy saying you're not good enough, pretty enough or worthy enough? Do you believe things that make you feel bad about yourself? These thoughts are not from Me but from the enemy who wants to destroy you. Ask Me to help you recognize when you are entertaining a lie so that you can immediately dismiss it. There will be trials that you may face, but you will face them with Me by your side. Some things you just can't do on your own strength, but I give you power to resist temptations. It is the same power that raised Jesus from the dead! Don't look at the situations you may face, but keep your eyes on Me and the promises I made to you in My Word. You can trust Me. I am unchanging. I will be by your side, always giving you everything you need. Will you let Me help you, My child?

But now thus says the Lord, he who created you, O Jacob, he who formed you,
O Israel: "Fear not, for I have redeemed you; I have called you by name, you are mine."
—Isaiah 43:1 (ESV)

I am your refuge when you dwell in Me and make Me your resting place. I am a safe place to lie down and place your head. My loving arms wrapped around you comfort and protect you and give you shelter. I undergird you and surround you like a fortress keeping you secure. When trouble comes, I am there rescuing and protecting. I am always with you in times of testing and guide your path. Come, let Me be your safe place.

The Lord is my shepherd, I shall not want. He makes me lie down in green pastures;
He leads me beside quiet waters. He restores my soul; He guides me in the paths of
righteousness for His name's sake. Even though I walk through the valley of the shadow
of death, I fear no evil, for You are with me; Your rod and Your staff, they comfort me.
You prepare a table before me in the presence of my enemies; You have anointed
my head with oil; My cup overflows. Surely goodness and lovingkindness will follow
me all the days of my life, And I will dwell in the house of the Lord forever.
—Psalm 23 (NASB)

MAY 12

$\mathcal{M}$y Word is your life source! It lights your way and gives you direction. You learn about My heart, who I am, My nature and character. I speak to you in the verses. You are My student, learning one on one! My Word is the truth and speaks My truth. It is free of error, reliable and doesn't contradict. I want you to use it for teaching, correcting and training others as well as for yourself. It is the perfect textbook! It will equip you for life! Cultivate a love and respect for My Word. Ask Me to help you with that. It is My treasured possession that I give to you.

All Scripture is God-breathed and is useful for teaching, rebuking, correcting and training in righteousness, so that the servant of God may be thoroughly equipped for every good work.
—2 Timothy 3:16-17

Your word is a lamp for my feet, a light on my path.
—Psalm 119:105

MAY 13

$\mathcal{M}$y Word can penetrate your heart and cause a change without leaving a scar. It can point out the flaws in another and at the same time can convict you of the same flaw. It is given by My inspiration. I breathed My life into it. Your faith is strengthened when you hear and obey My Word. It is truth and life! You can use My Word to fight off temptation like My Son did. It is pure and a shield to those that put their trust in it. My Word is priceless!

Consequently, faith comes from hearing the message,
and the message is heard through the word about Christ.
—Romans 10:17

Then Jesus was led by the Spirit into the wilderness to be tempted by the devil. After fasting forty days and forty nights, he was hungry. The tempter came to him and said, "If you are the Son of God, tell these stones to become bread." Jesus answered, "It is written: 'Man shall not live on bread alone, but on every word that comes from the mouth of God.'"
—Matthew 4:1-4

MAY 14

$\mathcal{D}$o you ever think about how you treat Me? Do you purposely do things that bring joy to My heart, or are you complaining when things don't go right? Do you put Me first in your life, or have you chosen man's wisdom and ways over true love for Me? Do you love and trust in Me enough that you will go where I lead you or are you looking at what it will do for you also? Do you know you can do things that are a comfort to Me? I don't need to be comforted because I am the source of all comfort, but I feel things just as you feel things. Do you ever think about how your actions make Me feel? If you have forgotten what I treasure, your life will not be filled with the joy that can only be found in Me. There is no condemnation in this, but as your Heavenly Father, I want what is best for you, My dearly loved child. As you ponder these questions and see the changes that you need to make, it is a good thing. Godly sorrow produces repentance.

Godly sorrow brings repentance that leads to salvation and leaves no regret, but worldly sorrow brings death.
—2 Corinthians 7:10

If we confess our sins, he is faithful and just and will forgive us our sins and purify us from all unrighteousness.
—1 John 1:9

MAY 15

$\mathcal{I}$ want you to desire what is precious in My sight. The world looks at outward beauty, but I look at the heart. What is in your heart is all that matters to Me. Are your motives for doing things pleasing to Me or are they more beneficial for you? Do you do what is right or succumb to fear? Are you guided by what the world says, or does My Word light your path? Sometimes you get swept up in the day's activities and forget what is important to Me. Remind yourself daily that what is in your heart is of great worth in My sight.

Your beauty should not come from outward adornment, such as elaborate hairstyles and the wearing of gold jewelry or fine clothes. Rather, it should be that of your inner self, the unfading beauty of a gentle and quiet spirit, which is of great worth in God's sight.
—1 Peter 3:3-4

MAY 16

$\mathcal{B}$e careful how you live your life. People watch what you say and do, even when you are not aware of it. You may be the only Bible they read! Your behavior may win someone over who does not know Me as they observe how you interact with them and how you handle and respond to situations. Being My example is a high calling. Please don't take that lightly. I am not calling you to do anything that I have not already equipped you for. You have everything you need for life and godliness because you have My power flowing through you. Remember that power and use it as you face situations where your initial response may be to react on your own strength, rather than respond in My power and love.

Wives, in the same way submit yourselves to your own husbands so that,
if any of them do not believe the word, they may be won over without words by
the behavior of their wives, when they see the purity and reverence of your lives.
—1 Peter 3:1-2

His divine power has granted to us everything pertaining to life and godliness,
through the true knowledge of Him who called us by His own glory and excellence.
—2 Peter 1:3 (NASB)

MAY 17

$\mathcal{I}$ listen as I hear people talking about others and it breaks My heart. I look into their hearts and see that the prime reason they do this is to build themselves up at the other person's expense. This should not be, for I detest this! Please be careful when talking about other people. Unless you are part of the solution, guard your tongue rather than tear them down. Find godly solutions. Lift them up to Me in prayer. Make it your goal to build people up. This is the better way and pleasing in My sight.

Do not let any unwholesome talk come out of your mouths, but only what is
helpful for building others up according to their needs, that it may benefit those who listen.
—Ephesians 4:29

Whoever derides their neighbor has no sense, but the one who has understanding holds
their tongue. A gossip betrays a confidence, but a trustworthy person keeps a secret.
—Proverbs 11:12-13

MAY 18

*L*ike Paul, you feel as if you have a "thorn in your flesh," something that is annoying at best and debilitating at worst. You repeatedly pray to Me for it to go away. But like Paul, I have left it there to show you a great lesson. I realize that in the world's eyes it doesn't seem easy or fair. But I am more concerned with your character than your comfort. That may sound harsh if you don't know My nature. My child, I provide comfort, strength and peace to see you through everything. My power is made perfect in weakness! Think on this: My power rests in you! The world cannot understand this. Through trials, you learn the skills to see you through hardships that will come in the future. Through trials you grow closer to Me. I really do want the best for you! If this is still hard for you to grasp, seek after Me. Ask Me to help you with this. I want you to have eyes to see My ways and to embrace them with all your heart so that you can boast like Paul that My grace is sufficient for you, for My power is made perfect in your weakness!

Therefore, in order to keep me from becoming conceited, I was given a thorn in my flesh, a messenger of Satan, to torment me. Three times I pleaded with the Lord to take it away from me. But he said to me, "My grace is sufficient for you, for my power is made perfect in weakness." Therefore I will boast all the more gladly about my weaknesses, so that Christ's power may rest on me. That is why, for Christ's sake, I delight in weaknesses, in insults, in hardships, in persecutions, in difficulties. For when I am weak, then I am strong.
—2 Corinthians 12:7b-10

MAY 19

*I*f you know Me, I have given you a spiritual gift. There are different kinds of gifts that I give to My children, but they all come from Me. Some are natural and some are supernatural, but all are used to strengthen and encourage others. Do you know the gift or gifts I have given you? If you do, keep using them and look for the opportunities I provide for you. If you don't know what gift you have been given, become aware of what the spiritual gifts are from My Word. Ask Me for guidance, see what comes naturally to you and actively pursue the gifts. You will be amazed at the lives you will touch and how good it makes you feel when you are using the spiritual gifts I gave you!

We have different gifts, according to the grace given to each of us. If your gift is prophesying, then prophesy in accordance with your faith; if it is serving, then serve; if it is teaching, then teach; if it is to encourage, then give encouragement; if it is giving, then give generously; if it is to lead, do it diligently; if it is to show mercy, do it cheerfully.   —Romans 12:6-8

*H*ave you heard My still small voice asking you to put it down? I am asking you to let go of whatever has so much importance connected to it, which is taking you away from Me. I see you struggling, wanting to be obedient, but also wanting the "idol" you treasure. It is a tough struggle. I do understand. Sometimes there is a blessing, not in what I give you but in what I take away! Try to look at this the way I see it. I have so much more in store for you, so much more to give you, but some things need to change in order for you to receive what I have for you. Put your faith in My plan for you and the blessing that comes with it!

For they themselves report what kind of reception you gave us.
They tell how you turned to God from idols to serve the living and true God.
—1 Thessalonians 1:9

I hate those who cling to worthless idols; as for me, I trust in the Lord.
—Psalm 31:6

*W*hen things seem to be out of control and there is no ending in sight, stand firm, rooted and grounded in My Word. My Word gives you guidance, direction and comfort. It opens your eyes to who I am and what I do for you on your behalf. Pause and wrap yourself in My love. Let Me give you insight and understanding. Allow My patience and perseverance to see you through this. Let what I see affect what you see; you can only see the situation, but I see from beginning to end and in between. My ways are different from your ways. I am more concerned with developing a godly character than with temporal things. Come, be surrounded by My loving support as you wait out the storm.

Be on your guard; stand firm in the faith; be courageous; be strong.
—1 Corinthians 16:13

Put on the full armor of God, so that you can take your stand against the devil's schemes.
—Ephesians 6:11

*T*here are times when I discipline My children. When I do it, My motivation is never out of anger or rejection. It is always out of total love. That may be hard for you to understand. You may have had an earthly parent who was overly strict or disciplined harshly or was even abusive. Please don't confuse Me with your earthly parents. I am the perfect Father, and I treat you like My children. My desire is for you to have complete wholeness, and there are times I need to offer correction for your own good because I love you! There may be things in your life that are holding you back or getting in the way. Once they are eliminated and you are healed, you will have an abundant life. I want so much for you to walk in victory!

My son, do not despise the Lord's discipline, and do not resent his rebuke,
because the Lord disciplines those he loves, as a father the son he delights in.
—Proverbs 3:11-12

"My son, do not make light of the Lord's discipline, and do not lose heart when he rebukes you,
because the Lord disciplines the one he loves, and he chastens everyone he accepts as his son."
—Hebrews 12:5b-6

*Y*ou are walking with Me and growing every day. You have given Me your life and are living for Me. That gives Me tremendous joy and great pleasure! Treasure that in your heart. My dear one, I am calling you to step out even further in faith and to say yes even when you might feel foolish. Taking the chance that may have you feeling a little foolish may be what is required to bring forth a miracle or healing in My name. Isn't it worth the risk? Look at the example of Moses. He was willing to look like a fool when I told him to put a tree into the bitter water in front of all the people with him. He obeyed and the bitterness vanished and the water became fit to drink! Think of the amazing things that are in store for you just by being open to saying yes!

Then Moses cried out to the Lord, and the Lord showed him a piece of wood.
He threw it into the water, and the water became fit to drink. There the Lord
issued a ruling and instruction for them and put them to the test.
—Exodus 15:25

I see your struggles with wanting to do everything right in order for Me to love you and in pushing yourself to do good things to earn My favor. When you don't do everything you feel you need to do, you think I am angry with you. Oh, My dear, dear child, that is such a lie. That lie comes from the enemy who seeks to destroy. You can't earn My love; it is already there unconditionally! There is nothing that you can do to take that love away. You are made right with Me and are righteous, not from what you do, but from what My Son did on the cross. I never come to condemn you; that is the enemy. I come to encourage you and build you up!

The Lord appeared to us in the past, saying: "I have loved you
with an everlasting love; I have drawn you with unfailing kindness."
—Jeremiah 31:3

But when the kindness and love of God our Savior appeared, he saved us,
not because of righteous things we had done, but because of his mercy.
He saved us through the washing of rebirth and renewal by the Holy Spirit.
—Titus 3:4-5

I love you with a love that will never end! There is nothing you can do to take that away. I see the things you do that aren't pleasing to Me, and sometimes you want to hide from Me while you choose to continue down that path. Please don't try to hide. You can't hide anyway, and I know that—deep down—you realize that. Your righteousness is based on what My Son did and not what you did or could do. I don't want you to feel condemnation or guilt especially when I am here ready to forgive you if you just repent and ask for forgiveness. Don't live with guilt or regret from your past. Give Me your failures and I will use them for your good and for My glory! There will come a time that the enemy can no longer torment you because you can counter his lies with My truth: that you are righteous in Me!

God made him who had no sin to be sin for us,
so that in him we might become the righteousness of God.
—2 Corinthians 5:21

We know that anyone born of God does not continue to sin;
the One who was born of God keeps them safe, and the evil one cannot harm them.
—1 John 5:18

MAY 26

I invite you to come into My presence today and everyday! Come and worship Me with a glad heart! I know you sometimes don't feel worthy, but My Son's blood has cleansed you. It is your honor and privilege as My child to be able to come to Me. Enter into My gates with thanksgiving and into My courts with praise! Think about all the things you are thankful for that came from My loving hands. I love spending time with you because I love you and enjoy your company. My love for you will last forever. I am never going away from you! Will you come and spend time with Me today?

Shout for joy to the Lord, all the earth. Worship the Lord with gladness;
come before him with joyful songs. Know that the Lord is God. It is He who made us,
and we are His; we are His people, the sheep of His pasture. Enter His gates with
thanksgiving and His courts with praise; give thanks to Him and praise His name. For the
Lord is good and His love endures forever; His faithfulness continues through all generations.
—Psalm 100

MAY 27

*S*ometimes you wonder if I can really provide what you need, if I can really heal what is wrong with your body, if I can really fix the situation you are in that seems impossible. Remember that I am Almighty God. Nothing is too difficult for Me. I am the God of possibilities. Keep your focus on this truth. I was here before all things were made. I formed the world and made all of creation. I am the God of all mankind. I am omnipotent, for there is no one greater. Keep your focus on who I am, not on what you wonder and question. Nothing is too hard for Me!

"I am the Lord, the God of all mankind. Is anything too hard for me?"
—Jeremiah 32:27

"I am the Alpha and the Omega," says the Lord God,
"who is, and who was, and who is to come, the Almighty."
—Revelation 1:8

MAY 28

*Y*ou hear people using bad language as they tell their crude jokes. You see moms being impatient with their whiny toddlers. You observe "church" people doing things that you know are not pleasing to Me. You desire to pray for these people and you ask Me what I see so you have greater insight into how to pray for them. My child, you will be surprised by My answer to you. What I see is someone who is judging and shouldn't be. That is not your place to judge, but Mine. I know this was not the response you were expecting. I also know you received it in the way it was intended, not condemning you in any way, but speaking truth and correction with love. I also know you will see that I am right and you will repent. You will also realize your intentions were good, but your motive was not. I will reveal to you that even though you didn't intentionally try it or were aware of it, your countenance had a "look" of judgment that they could observe. This hinders My work. I know that was not your intention My child, so please just show them love and let Me do the rest.

*Do not judge, or you too will be judged. For in the same way you judge others,
you will be judged, and with the measure you use, it will be measured to you.*
—Matthew 7:1-2

MAY 29

*W*hat are you really passionate about? I want you to be passionate about your godly interests and goals. But My greatest desire is that you have a burning passion to be more like My Son and His example to you. This is a goal that has eternal rewards. I want you to be passionate about learning to think like Jesus, to love like He does, and that you would desire His heart. You learn this by spending a lot of time with Him. This is what I want for you, learning first-hand from Jesus. Will you desire what I desire for you?

*"For the bread of God is the bread that comes down from heaven and gives life to the world."
"Sir," they said, "always give us this bread." Then Jesus declared, "I am the bread of life. Whoever comes to me will never go hungry, and whoever believes in me will never be thirsty."*
—John 6:33-35

*Jesus answered, "Everyone who drinks this water will be thirsty again,
but whoever drinks the water I give them will never thirst. Indeed, the water
I give them will become in them a spring of water welling up to eternal life."*
—John 4:13-14

*Y*our life has meaning. There are people watching you, learning from you and imitating you. Whether you realize it or want it, it is happening. Who is your example? Are you learning from Me and imitating Me? Are you doing what you see Me doing? You have the opportunity to be My light and love for others. I have equipped you for ministry. You don't have to actively do or say anything. Just live your life for Me. For some people, you may be the only Bible they see.

He has told you, O man, what is good; And what does the Lord require of you, but to do justice, to love kindness, and to walk humbly with your God.
—Micah 6:8 (NASB)

You, my brothers and sisters, were called to be free. But do not use your freedom to indulge the flesh; rather, serve one another humbly in love. For the entire law is fulfilled in keeping this one command: "Love your neighbor as yourself."
—Galatians 5:13-14

MAY 31

*W*hy do you hold on to your anger or carry a grudge? Why aren't you forgiving those that you feel have done you wrong? Have you ever taken the time to really ask why you are doing this? Is holding on to these things helping you in any way or making a difference? Is it really punishing the other person? Does it make you feel better, really? If you are truly being honest with yourself and let go of the temporary satisfaction you feel that is on the surface, you'll see that holding on to these things just makes you constantly feel bad inside. Holding on to these things is not My way. There is no permanent peace or contentment in that. I know it is hard for you to let go of these things. You can't do it and maintain it on your own strength. That's why My Son died for you. That power that raised Him up from the dead is the same power I give you to forgive and let go of anger and grudges. All you have to do is choose My way and repent of these actions. Then My strength in you will be doing the hard work. Instead of the temporary satisfaction, wouldn't you rather have peace that will last?

He who is slow to anger is better than the mighty, And he who rules his spirit, than he who captures a city.
—Proverbs 16:32 (NASB)

And when you stand praying, if you hold anything against anyone, forgive them, so that your Father in heaven may forgive you your sins.   —Mark 11:25

JUNE 1

*W*hat do you give priority to? Is it to make money, be entertained, enjoy the good life, or indulge in pleasure? It's so tempting, isn't it, especially from the world's perspective? But the happiness from these things is so fleeting and there is no enduring significance. My dear one, I want you to think as I think. Don't just focus on your time here on earth, but set your sights on eternity with Me! Give priority to things of eternal value rather than to things of this world. Be passionate about finding ways to be useful for My kingdom. Ask Me; I will gladly show you and give you tasks. Identify the spiritual gift I have given you. Make yourself available to people who need help and share the Good News about what I am doing in your life. You will be pleasantly surprised to find there is joy in reaching out to others. The rewards are far greater and last for eternity!

Each of you should use whatever gift you have received to serve others, as faithful stewards of God's grace in its various forms. If anyone speaks, they should do so as one who speaks the very words of God. If anyone serves, they should do so with the strength God provides, so that in all things God may be praised through Jesus Christ. To him be the glory and the power for ever and ever. Amen.
—1 Peter 4:10-11

For it is by grace you have been saved, through faith—and this is not from yourselves, it is the gift of God—not by works, so that no one can boast. For we are God's handiwork, created in Christ Jesus to do good works, which God prepared in advance for us to do.
—Ephesians 2:8-10

JUNE 2

*H*ow often do you try to be in control of a situation? Do you offer unsolicited advice to others on how to do something or how to solve a situation? Do you pray to Me and make suggestions on how things should be done? My child, your intentions are good but misguided. What you are really doing is trying to be Me! Let Me do My job because that is My rightful position and place. I see the big picture. I know the hearts of people. I move supernaturally. Your job is to pray. It is an important and powerful job that I want you to do and it moves Heaven and Earth.

Lord, I know that people's lives are not their own; it is not for them to direct their steps.
—Jeremiah 10:23

My son, give me your heart and let your eyes delight in my ways.
—Proverbs 23:26

JUNE 3

*W*hen you feel tired, worn out, overwhelmed, or discouraged, please don't focus your attention on how you are feeling. Make a mental shift. Recognize your weakness and celebrate it. You question what is there to celebrate. It is when you recognize you are weak and can't carry on in your own strength that you are free to turn to Me and draw from My strength and power, which are endless! When you make that connection to Me and feel My strength pour into you, you are revived, renewed and refreshed. That is something to be celebrated! Oh, My child, won't you turn to Me and let Me give you what you desire?

I will refresh the weary and satisfy the faint.

—Jeremiah 31:25

But he said to me, "My grace is sufficient for you, for my power is made perfect in weakness." Therefore I will boast all the more gladly about my weaknesses, so that Christ's power may rest on me.

—2 Corinthians 12:9

JUNE 4

*M*y love for you is relentless and unchanging. I will never give up on you no matter what you are going through. My love will always protect you. It has the capacity to take away all fear if you allow it. My love will always believe the best about you in every situation. I want so much to melt your heart so you receive the fullness of My love which is vast and immeasurable! I want to fill you with My love so you can see the world and people the way I do, through loving eyes of compassion. I want you to look past what the enemy puts in your path to cause you harm, so you can see Me on the other end with love that conquers all! Come, rest and abide in My love and in My promises!

And so we know and rely on the love God has for us. God is love. Whoever lives in love lives in God, and God in them.

—1 John 4:16

The steadfast love of the Lord never ceases; his mercies never come to an end; they are new every morning; great is your faithfulness.

—Lamentations 3:22-23 (ESV)

JUNE 5

*I*n this world, sadly, there will be trouble. Because of the fallen world, you will probably experience loss, emotional and physical pain and heartache. This was not My original plan. It grieves My heart to watch the consequences of the Fall. But My Son died to overcome the world! What that means to you is that you will not be tested with trials or temptations beyond what you are able to endure. You also have My promise of walking alongside you and pouring into you endless supplies of strength, peace, comfort and provision. I give a way of escape when the load gets to be too much. There may be trials that seem to rage against this promise, but hold on to My promise— that My grace is sufficient for every situation you face!

But he said to me, "My grace is sufficient for you, for my power is made perfect in weakness." Therefore I will boast all the more gladly about my weaknesses, so that Christ's power may rest on me.
—2 Corinthians 12:9

"I have told you these things, so that in me you may have peace. In this world you will have trouble. But take heart! I have overcome the world."
—John 16:33

JUNE 6

I never give up on you. I am right here when you are going through trials, pain, fear, sleepless nights and worries. Even though you may be straying, stagnant, or have put up barriers, I am here waiting patiently for you to come knocking at the door. I will not force you to come but only encourage you. If you open up to Me, I will come into your life. My spirit will live in you and you will partake of My divine nature and be transformed into My image. Do you know how amazing that is? If you don't fully understand what all that means, I will explain it all as you read My Word and as we walk through life together.

Here I am! I stand at the door and knock. If anyone hears my voice and opens the door, I will come in and eat with that person, and they with me.
—Revelation 3:20

Jesus answered, "I am the way and the truth and the life. No one comes to the Father except through me."
—John 14:6

*H*ow many times have you thrown out food because it was spoiled? Do you have any clothing in your closet that you don't wear, but you continue to go shopping for more? Do you have the need to have the latest gadgets and electronics? How many things do you own that you aren't even using? I ask you these things not to condemn you but to get you thinking. Do you know that people on the poverty level in the United States are considered wealthy in the eyes of most of the world? I want to awaken you to the problem of excess. Excess comes from the world's standards. This is not My standard though. Joy is not derived from having things. The happiness and satisfaction you get from acquiring things is fleeting and has no eternal value. My joy which is long-lasting and eternal comes from a constant relationship with Me and in knowing your identity as My child. It comes from doing Kingdom work. Will you chose the better way and experience real joy?

Do not love the world or anything in the world. If anyone loves the world, love for the Father is not in them. For everything in the world—the lust of the flesh, the lust of the eyes, and the pride of life—comes not from the Father but from the world. The world and its desires pass away, but whoever does the will of God lives forever.
—1 John 2:15-17

JUNE 8

*W*here is your peace? When you are upset and worried, do you come to Me first or only after you go through other options? I watch as you look elsewhere for answers, and it saddens My heart when you spend even one more minute not connected to My peace, I care about you that much! The world wants you to find other substitutes, but only the peace I offer you is genuine and long-lasting. The peace I give you isn't dependent on circumstances, but in believing My promises to you and trusting in Me. It is a peace that is yours no matter what you are going through.

You keep him in perfect peace whose mind is stayed on you, because he trusts in you.
—Isaiah 26:3 (ESV)

"For the mountains may depart and the hills be removed, but my steadfast love shall not depart from you, and my covenant of peace shall not be removed," says the Lord, who has compassion on you.
—Isaiah 54:10 (ESV)

$\mathcal{S}$ometimes you want to come to Me in prayer but hesitate. You don't want to bother Me or you don't want to waste your prayer on some minor ailment or problem. You want to save up your prayers for something major and serious. Sometimes you don't even want to ask Me because you weren't being "good" enough that day. My child, those thoughts are not from Me but are lies you are believing. The truth is, I want you to come to Me with everything. No problem or concern is too small. I love when you want to spend time with Me, for you are never a bother. My Son died on the cross to make you righteous in My sight. When I look at you, I don't see what you did that day. I see Christ in you! So come to Me with all your concerns and joys. Sit on My lap and spend some time with Me.

For I will forgive their wickedness and will remember their sins no more.
—Hebrews 8:12

But now in Christ Jesus you who once were far away
have been brought near by the blood of Christ.
—Ephesians 2:13

$\mathcal{I}$ am the heart of your heart. As you press into greater intimacy with Me, seeking to know My heart and wanting to feel what I feel in My heart, our hearts will begin to mesh. You will have a spirit to spirit and heart to heart experience with Me! This can only happen when you let go of yourself completely and desire Me with your whole being. Open your heart completely to Me without any reservations or fear. Then you will love as I love. You will understand how to love and what love truly is. You will even comprehend how much I love you! You will have the power and ability to love others exactly as I do, including the unlovable, the unlovely and those that have wronged you. You will have My heart, will see people the way I do, and be able to do what the world says is impossible. Come, intertwine your heart with Mine…

The world cannot accept him, because it neither sees him nor knows him.
But you know him, for he lives with you and will be in you.
—John 14:17b

Whoever does not love does not know God, because God is love.
—1 John 4:8

JUNE 11

$\mathcal{D}$o you find yourself wanting to have the last word in a conversation that gets a little heated? Do you give your opinions freely, even when not asked? Are you constantly defending your actions, even when it's not necessary? These are pretty common responses, but they are not pleasing to Me. They are all rooted in pride. I share this with you because I know you want to mature. When you are ready to let go of these things, I will help you. As a believer, you already have My Holy Spirit inside you and can connect to My power any time you want. Ask Me and I will reveal to you when you are about to do something that is prideful so you can refrain. Ask Me and I will take away your desire to do these kinds of things. I want to walk along side you and help you to learn, grow and mature.

When pride comes, then comes disgrace, but with the humble is wisdom.
—Proverbs 11:2 (ESV)

But he gives us more grace. That is why Scripture says:
"God opposes the proud but shows favor to the humble."
—James 4:6

JUNE 12

$\mathcal{D}$id you know I chose you before creation to be an adopted part of My family? Before I brought forth this world into existence, I saw you and chose you. Even way back then, I saw you some day saying yes to My Son's free gift to you from the cross. Your adoption into My family is nothing like an earthly adoption. You are My sons and daughters and joint heirs with Jesus, your older brother seated right by My side in Heaven! This is the amazing outcome of My Son dying and being raised again from the cross! You are My child and nothing can come between us. You inherit all I have and will spend eternity with Me. Even now, I see you holy and without blame. You have My power flowing in you, to love like I love. Step into your inheritance!

In him we were also chosen, having been predestined according to the plan of him who works out everything in conformity with the purpose of his will. When you believed, you were marked in him with a seal, the promised Holy Spirit, who is a deposit guaranteeing our inheritance until the redemption of those who are God's possession—to the praise of his glory.
—Ephesians 1:11a, 13b-14

JUNE 13

*M*y Word gives you direction for where I want to take you. It lights your path so you know where to go. It gives you encouragement when you are unsure and guidelines to keep you going straight so you don't veer off the path. My Word stands alone and lasts forever. Other things come and go but not My Word! It does not change and is timeless. There is nothing to compare it to for its wisdom and insight. In it, I speak directly to you and address every situation you face. I show you how to attain peace, rest, joy and contentment. No other book can do that! I place great value in this Book. Will you do that, too?

For, "All people are like grass, and all their glory is like the flowers of the field;
the grass withers and the flowers fall, but the word of the Lord endures forever."
And this is the word that was preached to you.

—1 Peter 1:24-25

Your word is a lamp for my feet, a light on my path.

—Psalm 119:105

JUNE 14

*Y*ou read My Word and know what it says. You know My promises to you and recite some of them by heart. Yet there is hesitation. You don't want to call it doubt, yet you subconsciously wonder if it is true. You have an easier time believing My promises are true for others and are less sure when it comes to yourself. You don't want to admit that you have doubts because you think you are letting Me down. The truth is, you aren't letting Me down. I love you and am concerned. I know your struggles and I want so much for you to have victory over them. Tell Me, why do you keep on doubting? You don't really know, do you? You have the head knowledge; that isn't the problem. The problem is that you don't have the heart knowledge. I want you to write these promises on your heart by choosing to simply believe that what I say is true. Just say it, even if the faith isn't there yet! The more you choose to believe, the more it will be written in your heart. I am encouraging you to operate in the highest form of faith—faith that takes Me at My word.

Then he said to Thomas, "Put your finger here; see my hands.
Reach out your hand and put it into my side. Stop doubting and believe."

—John 20:27

JUNE 15

*A*re there days you feel like you have been forgotten? That I have overlooked you or even neglected you? You are having trouble feeling My presence and so you start wondering if I am there even though you really do know better. Remember, My dear one, it is impossible for Me to forget you. That is one of My promises to you. You are engraved on the palms of My hands! I love you that much. Picture it; write it on your heart. Your name is written on My hand. Also remember, My Son's hands have the scars from the nails that were driven into Him as He thought of you. You are never forgotten! Remember what is written on My hands and My Son's hands, and draw encouragement and hope from that.

Can a mother forget the baby at her breast and have no compassion on the child she has borne? Though she may forget, I will not forget you! See, I have engraved you on the palms of my hands; your walls are ever before me.
—Isaiah 49:15-16

After the soldiers had nailed Jesus to the cross, they divided up his clothes into four parts, one for each of them.
—John 19:23a (CEV)

JUNE 16

*W*hy do you stay awake at night wondering about or worrying over a situation you face? You already know worrying is not going to help the situation improve. But you still continue to do it. You try very hard not to but the next moment you find yourself worrying again. My child, I want you to focus on what My Word says! I do not slumber. I am awake and watching over you all night long! I am in control of every situation and am aware of everything at all times. My solutions are so much better than what you can come up with because I know the whole picture and all those involved. Choose to focus on what I am doing rather than on the situation. Sweet dreams!

I lift up my eyes to the mountains—where does my help come from? My help comes from the Lord, the Maker of heaven and earth. He will not let your foot slip— he who watches over you will not slumber; indeed, he who watches over Israel will neither slumber nor sleep. The Lord watches over you— the Lord is your shade at your right hand; the sun will not harm you by day, nor the moon by night. The Lord will keep you from all harm— he will watch over your life; the Lord will watch over your coming and going both now and forevermore.
—Psalm 121

JUNE 17

*I*f you are being honest with yourself, am I really first in your life? Look at how you spend your time. Where do I fit into that? There is no condemnation; I just want to open your eyes. I know your intentions are good, but are they enough? Ask Me to take away your desire for anything that is taking the place of Me being first in your life. Ask Me to show you ways to take more time out of your busy day to connect with Me. Ask Me for help when you're not sure how to proceed. I want you to share with Me something that made you laugh, or just pause and be filled up with My strength and power when you are weary. Ask Me for fresh encounters and to increase your hunger for more. I will give you your heart's desires and you will be blessed!

*But if from there you seek the Lord your God, you will
find him if you seek him with all your heart and with all your soul.*
—Deuteronomy 4:29

I love those who love me, and those who seek me find me.
—Proverbs 8:17

JUNE 18

*W*hen you are facing a situation that crushes your very core and makes you feel like you are gasping for air and about to go under, or when you feel like your heart is being ripped out of you, cry out to Me, My dear child! Please don't continue in that wretched state. You don't have to. My Son died for this very reason. I am here to minister to you, for I am close to the brokenhearted. Allow Me to be in control as you consciously turn everything over to Me. Once you turn it over consciously, leave it with Me and don't take it back again. This decision may take work on your part as you may have to make that choice over and over again. I am right by your side. Cling tightly to My promises and to Me. I will help rescue and restore. You are not alone!

The Lord is close to the brokenhearted and saves those who are crushed in spirit.
—Psalm 34:18

*Have I not commanded you? Be strong and courageous. Do not be afraid;
do not be discouraged, for the Lord your God will be with you wherever you go.*
—Joshua 1:9

*F*ind comfort in Me and rest for your soul. My rest is different than the rest you get at night. My rest is not dependent on sleep. It is something I alone can give you. It penetrates tired, weary, worn out bodies and minds. It breathes new life, strength, security and stability into your innermost being. It cannot be shaken or taken away. The only way it can be removed is if you make that choice yourself. Come into your secret place and find Me! Open up your heart to draw Me in. Lay your head on My shoulder as I wrap My arms around you; and give you rest that penetrates your soul.

It is in vain that you rise up early and go late to rest,
eating the bread of anxious toil; for he gives to his beloved sleep.
—Psalm 127:2 (ESV)

Take my yoke upon you, and learn from me, for I am gentle
and lowly in heart, and you will find rest for your souls.
—Matthew 11:29 (ESV)

*M*y child, I long for an intimate relationship with you. Come, sit on My lap and spend time with Me. Tell Me about your day, just like you would tell your family at home. You have a home with Me, too. I'm your Abba Father, your Daddy! I love to hear about what excites you and about what troubles you. I want to hear when things didn't go as planned, the frustrations you have. Tell Me about your fears, your hopes and dreams. I care about everything! Yes, I already know what you will tell Me since I am all-knowing, but that's not the point. The point is, I care and want that relationship with you. The more time you spend with Me, the more you will be tuned in to hearing Me respond to what you say and ask. It is a special way of talking to you and unlike the way you hear from people around you. You will learn to hear Me if that is your heart's desire. Will you spend time with Me, My child?

The Lord your God is with you, the Mighty Warrior who saves. He will take great
delight in you; in his love he will no longer rebuke you, but will rejoice over you with singing.
—Zephaniah 3:17

*Y*ou feel as if life is hard and you are getting discouraged. You may be disappointed and even losing hope. No matter what comes your way, you do not have to be defeated. Cling to My promises when you have nothing else to hold on to. They are intended to give you direction, inspiration and hope! My intentions were never to have you walk alone through life without guidance or a purpose. I am faithful and keep My promises. I encourage you also to have a plan in place before a situation develops so you can go right to it without much thought. That plan should include coming to Me first, worshipping Me and sharing everything that is on your heart. Read and reread My promises and write them on your heart. Read My Word, especially the Psalms, and learn from David. Draw strength from worship music and other believers who can pray with you and give you wise counsel. You are never alone; and never forgotten!

*Keep me safe, my God, for in you I take refuge. I say to the Lord, "You are
my Lord; apart from you I have no good thing." You make known to me the path of life;
you will fill me with joy in your presence, with eternal pleasures at your right hand.*
—Psalm 16:1-2, 11

---

*M*y child, where is your joy? Do you come expectantly to find joy in Me? Is that something you seek daily? You may never really have experienced My joy or never really thought about it before. Something may have even taken your joy away from you. I want you to have it back. Seek joy with your heart, for it is attainable no matter what you face! Experiencing joy is a wonderful place to be. You will absolutely cherish it once you experience it. Joy is not dependent on anyone or on anything you have or do. Joy can only be found in Me. Have you ever allowed your heart to fully come into My presence? I ask that not in a condemning way but because I love you and want so much for you to experience My joy in your life. Come into My presence and you will find it. Let go of anything hindering that from happening, which might be past hurts, hardships, pride, strongholds, or lies you believe. Choose to let them all go. Open all of your heart and let Me in; it is then you will find My joy. Stay connected to My presence to keep that joy. I want you to experience a joy-filled life in Me. Will you choose to receive it?

Rejoice in the Lord always. I will say it again: Rejoice!   —Philippians 4:4

JUNE 23

*Y*ou feel My presence during your quiet time and as you are worshiping. You find this to be a wonderful experience, but there is so much more I want to awaken you to! I don't just want it to be a wonderful experience or event that happens once in a while or even daily. I want you to abandon everything and stay with Me in your heart of hearts. Become continuously aware of My presence and be content living there. You do this by guarding your heart and mind in what you allow in and by pursuing everything about Me. Constantly fill your mind and heart with more of Me. I want to give you an overwhelming revelation of My heart to your heart so that you reflect My glory and live out of there and share My love with others. It is your choice. It's a whole new way of thinking. I want you to live in My presence. Are you ready for an amazing, changed life?

You, God, are my God, earnestly I seek you; I thirst for you, my whole being longs for you, in a dry and parched land where there is no water.
—Psalm 63:1

My son, pay attention to what I say; turn your ear to my words. Do not let them out of your sight, keep them within your heart; for they are life to those who find them and health to one's whole body. Above all else, guard your heart, for everything you do flows from it.
—Proverbs 4:20-23

JUNE 24

*D*o you struggle with eating or drinking habits? I am concerned that you are using food and drink for purposes that aren't pleasing to Me. Become aware if you are using them as a reward, or when you are bored or stressed, or out of habit when you're watching TV, or as a temporary escape from problems. None of these reasons is good if done continually. You are substituting these things for getting your fulfillment in Me. They are all a temporary pleasure, but I offer you a long-lasting one. I can give you all you need to make the changes. You have My power to resist temptation if you grab hold of it. I can take away your desire for food and drink when it is not beneficial to you if you just ask Me. Let Me help you. I will walk with you on this journey.

The eye is the lamp of the body. If your eyes are healthy, your whole body will be full of light.
—Matthew 6:22

But I discipline my body and keep it under control, lest after preaching to others I myself should be disqualified.
—1 Corinthians 9:27 (ESV)

*Y*ou hear the news of terrorists, violence, murders and of discord in the government. You are concerned about how you will pay your bills. You wonder about your future and that of your children. Sometimes your concern turns to worry and panic. You already know worrying doesn't help the situation at all, yet you can't help yourself. My child, there are things you have no control over. It is in these times I want you to turn to Me. Even though the situation may remain, I can help you change the way you look at things and react to them. You are only seeing one part of the situation, but I see it in its entirety. Ask Me to show you what I am doing and what the world can't see. Trust that I am at work in every situation and look for it. Keep your focus on Me, what I am doing and what I can give you. Even in the midst of your uncertainty, I can give you My peace which is not dependent on any circumstance and is long lasting. You have the choice of focusing on the situation or on Me. Won't you choose the better way?

I sought the Lord, and he answered me; he delivered me from all my fears.
—Psalm 34:4

When I am afraid, I put my trust in you.

—Psalm 56:3

*D*o you have joy in your life? Come seek Me, for I am the source of all joy! I am full of joy, and I give it freely. As you come to the end of yourself and seek Me with your whole being, it is then you will come into My presence and find joy. Nothing in life can give you joy that lasts. Everything is fleeting. My joy not only lasts, but you can experience it no matter what you are going through in your life. Come, receive My joy!

A cheerful heart is good medicine, but a crushed spirit dries up the bones.
—Proverbs 17:22

Until now you have not asked for anything in my name.
Ask and you will receive, and your joy will be complete.

—John 16:24

JUNE 27

*H*ave you ever wondered what it means to be My adopted child? It will mean everything to you once you fully understand! Your inheritance is everything I own, all the spiritual riches that are in My Son, both for now and for eternal life! They are the things that truly matter, not what the world thinks is important. Your citizenship is now different, too. You are a citizen of heaven, your true home. You have the right to be called a Christian. Being your Father, I am your caregiver and with loving authority over you, I offer correction and discipline to help you; it is never out of anger. I am the perfect Father, infinitely patient, wise and loving unconditionally. Because of My Son's work on the cross, I am not the condemning judge but the loving Father who forgives! I am not a long-distance Dad but am always by your side and accessible, desiring a close relationship with you. Live out of this knowledge of being My child and this new life you have!

See what great love the Father has lavished on us,
that we should be called children of God! And that is what we are!
—1 John 3:1a

JUNE 28

*B*eing My child changes the relationships you have with people. Jesus is your brother. Did you ever think of Him in this way? Your relationship with other believers changes, too. They are all your brothers and sisters because you all have the same Father. Your family has grown considerably. Your relationship with non-believers is different now, and you still want them to become part of your family. Continue to be a witness and show My love to them and pray for them because I want them to make the choice to be My children, too. I won't give up wanting them to come to Me. Your interests have changed also and are no longer self-centered or the same as the world but are centered on doing what will bring Me glory. Being My child gives you a different perspective on people and the way you live your life. Embrace your reality and destiny!

For those God foreknew he also predestined to be conformed to the image
of his Son, that he might be the firstborn among many brothers and sisters.
—Romans 8:29

And we all, who with unveiled faces contemplate the Lord's glory, are being transformed
into his image with ever-increasing glory, which comes from the Lord, who is the Spirit.
—2 Corinthians 3:18

JUNE 29

*Y*ou are My child, and I promise you that you will never be an orphan. You will always have a home with Me as your loving Father. The home I give you is a place of refuge and security— a place of kindness, warmth and love. When you are having a bad day or nothing seems to be going well, you can come to Me and sit on My lap and pour out your frustrations, worries and concerns. I will listen with compassion and will care about your feelings. When people turn on you, speak unkindly or do something to hurt you, I am always here to tell you how much I love you, value you and affirm you. You can trust Me; I am not going anywhere and I will always love you unconditionally.

God is our refuge and strength, a very present help in trouble. Therefore we will not fear though the earth gives way, though the mountains be moved into the heart of the sea, though its waters roar and foam, though the mountains tremble at its swelling.
—Psalm 46:1-3 (ESV)

It is good to give thanks to the Lord, to sing praises to your name, O Most High; to declare your steadfast love in the morning, and your faithfulness by night.
—Psalm 92:1-2 (ESV)

JUNE 30

I watch you, as your loving Father and see the pain you are in. I watch as you deal with the hurt you are feeling, the betrayal, disappointments and resentments. Instead of coming to Me to tell Me all about it, to lay everything at My feet and to receive My loving embrace, you choose a different path. You are frozen in comforting yourself with consuming anger, bitterness, control and isolation. Oh, My child, it grieves Me to see you this way. Choosing to stay stalled in these damaging emotions will not help you or the situation. Come to Me and choose to let go of everything. Let Me fill you with My endless love, compassion and understanding. Let Me empower you to forgive and let go. Won't you choose the better way?

Jesus answered, "I am the way and the truth and the life. No one comes to the Father except through me."
—John 14:6

Strive for peace with everyone, and for the holiness without which no one will see the Lord. See to it that no one fails to obtain the grace of God; that no "root of bitterness" springs up and causes trouble, and by it many become defiled.
—Hebrews 12:14-15 (ESV)

*Y*ou have done things that you regret and feel guilty about. Sometimes I see that you have a worldly sorrow about these things. That is not a good sorrow to have. It makes you feel remorse and is focused on self, how you got caught, and what other people will think. This will drag you back to your past actions and focus on the past. You also turn away from Me. Because you are ashamed and don't have a clear conscience, you shy away thinking I am mad at you. Let Me show you a better way! Instead of having a worldly sorrow, I want you to have a godly sorrow. This kind of sorrow produces repentance without regret. You realize that you have offended Me so you turn away from your sin, asking for My forgiveness and then turn to Me and My ways. The guilt you feel here is guilt over the sin and of offending and hurting Me. Godly sorrow leads to total freedom from guilt and a life pursuing what is pleasing to Me.

Even if I caused you sorrow by my letter, I do not regret it. Though I did regret it—I see that my letter hurt you, but only for a little while—yet now I am happy, not because you were made sorry, but because your sorrow led you to repentance. For you became sorrowful as God intended and so were not harmed in any way by us. Godly sorrow brings repentance that leads to salvation and leaves no regret, but worldly sorrow brings death.
—2 Corinthians 7:8-10

*W*hat occupies most of your thought life? Become aware of what you are thinking about. If you ask Me, I can help you become aware of your thoughts. Any thoughts that cause you to be unsettled or stressed, disregard them immediately. Get into the habit of rejecting any thoughts that are not centered on Me and being in My presence. It takes some time to cultivate this habit, but it surely makes your life calmer. When you watch what is going on in the world and feel heaviness, turn your attention quickly to Me to find peace. Don't live impressed with the enemy and his work on this earth. Focus on what I am doing instead. Think about things that are uplifting and praiseworthy. It will make a difference in your life!

Finally, brothers and sisters, whatever is true, whatever is noble, whatever is right, whatever is pure, whatever is lovely, whatever is admirable if anything is excellent or praiseworthy—think about such things.
—Philippians 4:8

$\mathcal{M}$y child, I see that you have fallen into a dark place— a place so dark and deep you don't know the way out and aren't sure there is one. Instead of turning to Me or reaching out to others, you have turned inward, shutting out the very ones who can help you. I know that it is hard to force yourself out of this darkness for help. But I know that you know Me and you know My promises, but they are foggy to you right now. I give you My strength and power to turn to Me right now. Please do it! Sing songs to Me, read the Psalms and learn from David who also felt as you do but who also found his way out, as you will. Reach out to someone who will pray with you and speak My promises into your life. I have plans for you, My child—plans to prosper you and not to harm you, plans to give you hope and a future. Believe it. I'm not giving up on you because I love you! Choose to believe Me. Choose to be in My light. Choose life in Me. Choose it now and never look back. This is a new day!

Cast all your anxiety on him because he cares for you.   —1 Peter 5:7

Likewise the Spirit helps us in our weakness. For we do not know what to pray for
as we ought, but the Spirit himself intercedes for us with groanings too deep for words.
—Romans 8:26 (ESV)

$\mathcal{C}$ome abide in My presence at nighttime. Let Me show you how. As you lie in bed, think of Me. Give Me your affection in worship, in singing and in just spending time with Me. Give Me your heart until My heart touches yours. As you wake up in the middle of the night, keep the heart connection going. Picture Me sitting by your bed and holding your hand. Picture Me keeping watch over you while you sleep. Wake up in the morning still connected to Me. Watch how it will affect your day as you learn to develop this habit.

On my bed I remember you; I think of you through the watches of the night. Because you
are my help, I sing in the shadow of your wings. I cling to you; your right hand upholds me.
—Psalm 63:6-8

JULY 5

*Y*ou partake of My communion meal as a perpetual remembrance of what My Son did for you. He was the perfect Lamb without blemish, and He gave himself willingly with you in His thoughts as He hung on the cross for your sins to be forgiven. He did it to give you complete access to Me and to be able to feel and receive My blessing. He did it to give you healing, wholeness and newness of life. When you come to My table, come with a repentant heart. Ask Me to show you areas of your life that may not be pleasing to Me so you can acknowledge them and ask for forgiveness. Come with a mindset of remembrance, honor and thanksgiving. Come with a mindset of receiving a changed life. As you partake of communion, open your spiritual eyes to what is happening that you hadn't been aware of before. It is a very powerful moment as you live your life accessing My power and love through this act of remembrance.

The Lord Jesus, on the night he was betrayed, took bread, and when he had given thanks, he broke it and said, "This is my body, which is for you; do this in remembrance of me." In the same way, after supper he took the cup, saying, "This cup is the new covenant in my blood; do this, whenever you drink it, in remembrance of me."
—1 Corinthians 11:23b-25

JULY 6

*Y*ou are aware of healings taking place and answers to prayers. You see the wonders of rainbows and brilliant sunsets. Throughout the week you see My hand at work in you and also in others. But I ask you, where is your awe and wonder? Where is your excitement about all these things? Have you become indifferent? I want to encourage you to change the way you process and think about things. Acknowledge what I am doing by stopping a moment, reflecting on it and getting excited. Don't you do it all the time when your sports team wins, when you find money between the seat cushions, or when someone gives you a bag of chocolate? Won't you do the same, or better, for what I do for you? It's a new mindset I want you to have.

For the heart of this people has become dull, with their ears they scarcely hear, and they have closed their eyes. Otherwise they would see with their eyes, hear with their ears, and understand with their heart and return, and I would heal them.
—Matthew 13:15 (NASB)

You have seen many things, but you do not observe them; Your ears are open, but none hears.
—Isaiah 42:20 (NASB)

JULY 7

*Y*ou have experienced disappointment in the past and probably will experience it in the future, too. How do you handle disappointment? Do you think about it and let it overwhelm you? That is the world's way and the most common way. But that is not My way. I want you to see things the way I see them. Did you ever think that it was really in your best interest and that I was protecting you from something I am able to see but you can't see? You are able to learn skills from this experience to help you the next time you are faced with a similar circumstance. Instead of wallowing in self-pity at the loss of a dream, which is so easy to do, you have the opportunity to search for the good and grab onto it, which is very important to do. You're learning important life skills and also building character which is important to Me and dear to My heart. I don't ask you to do anything that I haven't already equipped you to do. Try My approach as I walk by your side, cheering you on.

*"For my thoughts are not your thoughts, neither are your ways my ways,"
declares the Lord. "As the heavens are higher than the earth, so are my ways
higher than your ways and my thoughts than your thoughts."*

—Isaiah 55:8-9

JULY 8

*H*ow do you approach or look at life? Do you see the glass half full or half empty? Do you focus on what could go wrong or the worst that could happen? That is not My way. Place your focus on seeing My goodness and succeeding. Let this be your mindset regardless of your circumstances. I am on your side and empower you with everything you need for life and godliness. Make the conscious decision to look for the positive, knowing I am for you and giving you all you need. My outcome may be different from the outcome you wanted, but I see the whole picture and want what is best for you. You will have to trust Me on this. The more you know who I am, the easier it will become to trust Me. Come, see things the way I see them!

I can do all this through him who gives me strength.

—Philippians 4:13

So we can confidently say, "The Lord is my helper; I will not fear; what can man do to me?"

—Hebrews 13:6 (ESV)

JULY 9

*Y*ou end your prayers with "in Jesus name." Do you know what it means to pray in My Son's name and the impact it has? I know you use this ending all the time, and I wanted to bring attention to it because it really does mean something important. It means praying with My authority and power and asking Me to act upon your prayer. You are praying according to My will and I listen to you. It is not a magic formula guaranteeing the answer you asked for. If it is not for My glory and according to My will, ending the prayer this way is meaningless. It's not the words that matter but the purpose behind the prayer. May these not be just rote words you say. Recall the impact these words have as you say them.

And I will do whatever you ask in my name, so that the Father may be glorified in the Son. You may ask me for anything in my name, and I will do it.
—John 14:13-14

Then Jesus came to them and said, "All authority in heaven and on earth has been given to me."
—Matthew 28:18

JULY 10

*M*y Word has power and can transform your life! There are truths that are deeply personal to you. When you come to a passage that is speaking to you, meditate on it and write it on your heart. May it become indelible on your heart of hearts so that when trials come up, you have something to hold onto that will feed your soul, that will comfort and sustain you and give you hope. Read it with awe and wonder and fresh excitement! Find nuggets that change how you think and how you handle situations. My Word enhances and brings life to your world!

Keep this Book of the Law always on your lips; meditate on it day and night, so that you may be careful to do everything written in it. Then you will be prosperous and successful.
—Joshua 1:8

"Is not my word like fire," declares the Lord, "and like a hammer that breaks a rock in pieces?"
—Jeremiah 23:29

JULY 11

When you are going a million directions at once, when deadlines are looming, or when you don't know what to tackle first and you are just overwhelmed, stop and quiet yourself. Take a moment and just breathe. Breathe Me in. Breathe in all I have for you for this moment in time. Breathe in My power and goodness. Connect with Me and feel My calm and peace flow through you. Take one step at a time. Do one thing at a time. And remember, I am right by your side, providing all you need.

Jesus looked at them and said, "With man this is impossible, but with God all things are possible."

—Matthew 19:26

Behold, we consider those blessed who remained steadfast. You have heard of the steadfastness of Job, and you have seen the purpose of the Lord, how the Lord is compassionate and merciful.

—James 5:11 (ESV)

JULY 12

When you are completely broken emotionally, physically, or mentally, when there is nowhere else to go, and when you think it can't get any worse, come to Me. Put your faith and trust in Me. I can take the pieces of your life and put them back again into a solid, whole and healthy person. I will heal your heart and forgive your sins if you are truly sorry and want to turn away from this old life. Learn from Me and follow My ways. As you see what I can do, you will learn that the next time you can come to Me first and not as the last resort. My child, I'm glad you learned this lesson. Pass it on to others who need Me too!

All that the Father gives Me will come to Me, and the one who comes to Me I will certainly not cast out.

—John 6:37 (NASB)

I will not leave you as orphans; I will come to you.

—John 14:18

JULY 13

*D*o you have any idea how much I value you? You are of such great worth to Me! I created and formed you in your mother's womb. I gave you your unique personality, your likes and dislikes. I took such careful thought as to exactly how I wanted you to look and act. I put My whole heart and very soul into creating you! I look at you, whom I created and step back in awe and wonder. You are My masterpiece of which I am so proud! Receive My thoughts about you and write them on your heart. Do not let the world or people tell you differently. They do not think as I think or see what I see. Do not believe any lies that are contrary to these truths. There is nothing you have to do to earn My love. My love for you is simply there, unconditionally, and will never go away. Receive My love, My precious child!

For you created my inmost being; you knit me together in my mother's womb.
I praise you because I am fearfully and wonderfully made; your works are wonderful,
know that full well. My frame was not hidden from you when I was made in the secret place,
when I was woven together in the depths of the earth. Your eyes saw my unformed body;
all the days ordained for me were written in your book before one of them came to be.
—Psalm 139:13-16

JULY 14

*D*o you know that I am pursuing you and desire a relationship with you? I know you may be thinking, "How could He want to spend time with Me when He has all the prayers of the world to hear and answer?" You might even be afraid to let Me in completely because you're thinking that if I would really get to know you, I would decide this relationship isn't a good idea. You also may not be able to imagine that I could be that sold out for you. These are lies that you are believing. The truth is, I know all about you; I know all your thoughts and things done in secret. I know when you are smiling on the outside but crying on the inside. I love you, not because of who you are, but in spite of who you are. My love is based on My character and nature, not on yours. I love you with a passion and a purpose. I will never stop pursuing you! The question is, "Will you allow Me in and to transform your life?"

"This is the covenant I will make with the people of Israel after that time,"
declares the Lord. "I will put my law in their minds and write it on their
hearts. I will be their God, and they will be my people."
—Jeremiah 31:33

JULY 15

I know you are hard on yourself and only see what your mind allows. But I see the potential. I see the greatness in you. I want to call it out and awaken you to your destiny and purpose. I see the polished gem inside the unfinished exterior. I go to great lengths to polish you and bring out the goodness just waiting to come out. I see the finished work of My Son inside you. Let go of the lies you believe. I want you to see yourself the way I see you. Step into who you are and start living out of there.

You were taught, with regard to your former way of life, to put off your old self, which is being corrupted by its deceitful desires; to be made new in the attitude of your minds; and to put on the new self, created to be like God in true righteousness and holiness.
—Ephesians 4:22-24

Therefore, if anyone is in Christ, the new creation has come: The old has gone, the new is here!
—2 Corinthians 5:17

JULY 16

*Y*ou see yourself repeating the same mistakes over and over again. At times your thoughts can be destructive to you as you continue to believe the lies that swirl around in your mind. You sometimes stray from Me or become stagnant. You get discouraged and are hard on yourself. Oh, My child, I don't see you that way. I see the child I created so perfectly. I know your heart even when it doesn't match up with what you show on the outside. My Son willingly gave up His life because you were worth it. You are worth fighting for. I want to transform you into what I see and know and love. The work may be painful at times but I am right by your side helping you and cheering you on. I couldn't love you more, even the way you are right now. But I want you to be everything I created you to be. Will you let Me help you become who I see and love?

Some of the wise will stumble, so that they may be refined, purified and made spotless until the time of the end, for it will still come at the appointed time.
—Daniel 11:35

I am the true vine, and my Father is the gardener. He cuts off every branch in me that bears no fruit, while every branch that does bear fruit he prunes so that it will be even more fruitful. If you remain in me and I in you, you will bear much fruit; apart from me you can do nothing.
—John 15:1-2, 5b

JULY 17

I know you have been wronged and are upset, angry and bitter. My child, please don't stay there even though everything inside of you wants to. I know that harboring unforgiveness in your heart only brings destruction. It may give you temporary satisfaction to hold a grudge, but deep down it eats away at you over time. It also opens the door for the enemy to get a foothold in your life. It has no effect on the person who wronged you, only on you. You say forgiveness is just too hard and feel that you earned the right to hold on to the offense. You can choose to stay there, but it will only bring you harm. You are incapable of forgiving on your own strength. It takes a surrendered life and My spirit in you to be able to forgive. The hardest part is choosing to forgive. After you choose My plan for you, I give you the power and the ability to let go of the anger and to let go of the thoughts that you keep dwelling on concerning the situation. It is hard work at first but does get better as you continue to let go of the emotions and negative thoughts. You will find a release, a freedom and a peace; and that is a far better place to be. Come follow Me and make the choice to forgive. I will be by your side encouraging you.

Therefore, as God's chosen people, holy and dearly loved, clothe yourselves with compassion, kindness, humility, gentleness and patience. Bear with each other and forgive one another if any of you has a grievance against someone. Forgive as the Lord forgave you.
—Colossians 3:12-13

JULY 18

I value you because you are of great worth to Me. I see you as a wonderful treasure. When you are lost, I come searching for you. I would go to any length to bring you back to Me. Even when you backslide, I am right there waiting patiently for you to come home. I never give up on you or turn My back on you. I never think bad thoughts about you. I am there encouraging you and staying right by your side waiting for you to reach out to Me!

Then Jesus told them this parable: Suppose one of you has a hundred sheep and loses one of them. Doesn't he leave the ninety-nine in the open country and go after the lost sheep until he finds it? And when he finds it, he joyfully puts it on his shoulders and goes home. Then he calls his friends and neighbors together and says, 'Rejoice with me; I have found my lost sheep.'
—Luke 15:3-6

JULY 19

*H*ave you ever felt desperate, that there is no way out or no end in sight? It is at these times that you feel doubt and fear. You keep repeating these thoughts over and over and they are paralyzing you. But they are total lies. Stop these thoughts and purposefully turn your thoughts to Me. Declare that you believe in Me and in My promises to you. Let your faith be multiplied as you recall past times when I walked you through the storm. Declare that I will not fail you or leave you stranded. Declare that I speak the truth. Suddenly the weight is lifted as you turn your attention to where it needs to stay. Watch as these declarations come to fruition.

May the God of hope fill you with all joy and peace as you trust in him,
so that you may overflow with hope by the power of the Holy Spirit.
—Romans 15:13

JULY 20

*Y*ou have prayed the Lord's Prayer many times. Do you ever really stop to think about what you are saying and if you are doing what you are saying? You pray for My kingdom to come and My will to be done on earth as it is in Heaven. Do you know what that really means? You are to be My carriers of Heaven here on earth, demonstrating My will by healing in My name, ministering to others, loving as I love and sharing My Good News and promises. I want you to bring to life the revelation of what I wanted you to do all along. You have My power and authority to do these things in My name. Be a major part of bringing Heaven to earth. May these not just be words you recite, but bring them to life!

"This, then, is how you should pray: Our Father in heaven, hallowed be your name,
your kingdom come, your will be done, on earth as it is in heaven. Give us today
our daily bread. And forgive us our debts, as we also have forgiven our debtors.
And lead us not into temptation, but deliver us from the evil one."
—Matthew 6:9-13

JULY 21

*I*n My Word I share with you a model of how to pray. You say the words, "Hallowed be Your name." Have you ever thought about these words and what they mean? To hallow My name is to set it apart, to keep it holy, to honor it and for My name to never be associated with that which is common or profane. My name is powerful and mighty. Miracles, healings, signs and wonders are done in My name! It is something to be worshiped and revered. Keeping the holiness of My name before you causes you to have a proper view of yourself as you come before Me. It is only through My Son that I see you as righteous, not from anything you do. I encourage you to think about whether My name is being hallowed as you go about your life.

Do not swear falsely by my name and so profane the name of your God. I am the Lord.
—Leviticus 19:12

Ascribe to the Lord the glory due his name; worship the Lord in the splendor of his holiness.
—Psalm 29:2

JULY 22

*T*here is a time for everything. Generations come and go. Past generations are forgotten in this world. Past titles and positions of honor are recalled no more and have no merit. This is not how I see things. I see the whole picture from creating you with My own hands to where you will be for eternity. How you live your life on earth matters—not for the praises of man but for My glory! I watch how you live your life and whether you are choosing to do things because it is pleasing to Me and in My will. The world doesn't see these things, but I do. The world may consider these things unimportant, but they hold great importance in My sight. How will you choose to live your life and be remembered?

Serve wholeheartedly, as if you were serving the Lord, not people.
—Ephesians 6:7

Do not love the world or anything in the world. If anyone loves the world,
love for the Father is not in them. For everything in the world—the lust of the flesh,
the lust of the eyes, and the pride of life—comes not from the Father but from the world.
The world and its desires pass away, but whoever does the will of God lives forever.
—1 John 2:15-17

JULY 23

*A*t times you find yourself depleted, unsure of what is next, disillusioned and searching. I am the refreshment that you need! Turn to Me and give Me your questioning heart. Give Me your life and turn away from what hinders. I want to fill you with new seeds of hope and a purpose that will be planted deep and will take root. I will provide for you a stream of living water to refresh and nourish you. It will give you insight and direction. Drink from My refreshing water. Stay here a while as you get recharged and renewed. Watch what I do and learn from Me. Be filled!

He refreshes my soul. He guides me along the right paths for his name's sake.
—Psalm 23:3

I keep my eyes always on the Lord. With him at my right hand, I will not be shaken. Therefore my heart is glad and my tongue rejoices; my body also will rest secure, because you will not abandon me to the realm of the dead, nor will you let your faithful one see decay. You make known to me the path of life; you will fill me with joy in your presence, with eternal pleasures at your right hand.
—Psalm 16:8-11

JULY 24

*Y*ou have sacrificed a lot through the years. You feel that no one has noticed or really cared what you did. You feel that it didn't really matter and you even think, "What was the use?" What you are doing is listening and believing lies. My child, it does matter. It matters to Me! You aren't seeing what I see. You might not be seeing the fruition yet and you may never see it. What you have done and are doing is more important to Me than the outcome you want. Your sacrifice is a pleasing aroma to Me. Regardless of the outcome, continue giving your all. Receive My blessing!

In everything I did, I showed you that by this kind of hard work we must help the weak, remembering the words the Lord Jesus himself said: "It is more blessed to give than to receive."
—Acts 20:35

But seek first his kingdom and his righteousness, and all these things will be given to you as well.
—Matthew 6:33

JULY 25

*Y*ou were predestined to be conformed to the image of My Son. That's who you are! That is your identity and My plan for your life. When you look into a mirror, who do you see? I want you to look in the mirror and see Jesus in you. You are a new creation. Grow into it. Learn from Me and from My Word. Start living out of your identity. Fill your heart with the knowledge of who you are in Me. The more you know and love Me, the greater your willingness will be to trust and obey what I am calling you and equipping you to do. Step into it and own it!

For those God foreknew he also predestined to be conformed to the image of his Son, that he might be the firstborn among many brothers and sisters. And those he predestined, he also called; those he called, he also justified; those he justified, he also glorified.
—Romans 8:29-30

Follow my example, as I follow the example of Christ.   —1 Corinthians 11:1

JULY 26

*W*hen you look at your life, do you feel as if you are striving? Do you feel you may be completely on your own with no support? Do you feel drained and just not at peace? Tell Me My child, are you living for heaven or from heaven? When you are living for heaven, you will experience these things. You are living from a place that is depleting you. Take a new path, begin to live from Heaven and step into what is already a part of you. You are empowered to do what I am calling you to do. I have already given you exactly what you need. You will operate out of My resources and out of My strength, wisdom and direction. You are being obedient to My will, not yours. There is no striving; just walk in what is already laid out before you and trust in My provision. Choose to live from heaven, not for heaven.

But he said to me, "My grace is sufficient for you, for my power is made perfect in weakness." Therefore I will boast all the more gladly about my weaknesses, so that Christ's power may rest on me.
—2 Corinthians 12:9

The Lord makes firm the steps of the one who delights in him; though he may stumble, he will not fall, for the Lord upholds him with his hand.
—Psalm 37:23-24

JULY 27

*H*ave you ever been discouraged and thought, "What's the use?" Are you at a place where you don't see an end in sight nor any kind of solution that would fix the problem? Have you lost all hope on things working out? My dear one, those are all lies you are believing. My Son died so that you no longer have to lose hope! I am the God of hope. Please trust that this is My promise to you. As you purposefully trust in Me, your thoughts will turn to Me and what I will do for you. I will give you fresh insight and direction. I give you patience and perspective. I fill you with all joy and peace as you keep your focus on Me. Hope will return and be overflowing.

May the God of hope fill you with all joy and peace as you trust in him,
so that you may overflow with hope by the power of the Holy Spirit.

—Romans 15:13

Be joyful in hope, patient in affliction, faithful in prayer.

—Romans 12:12

JULY 28

*L*et Me fill you afresh. Let Me revive your spirit. Let Me awaken you to possibilities you haven't ever considered before and those you aren't even aware of. Let Me give you fresh insight into what I am doing because I want you to be part of it. I want to do a new work in you. Please allow Me in. Let Me be in control of all of you, of your entire life! I will not hurt or disappoint you but will give your life new meaning and purpose to be used for My glory. My spirit lives in you, guiding and equipping you. It's a wonderful life I have planned for you! Will you join Me and what I'm doing in you?

For it is God who works in you to will and to act in order to fulfill his good purpose.

—Philippians 2:13

Forget the former things; do not dwell on the past. See, I am doing a new thing! Now it springs
up; do you not perceive it? I am making a way in the wilderness and streams in the wasteland.

—Isaiah 43:18-19

JULY 29

When things go wrong, you want the quick fix. You just want the situation to be resolved without having to do anything to bring about a resolution. That is not My way. I want to come beside you and teach you. I give you insight and the skills needed to take a step. This is so you can build on what you are learning for the next insight and skill. I want to mold, shape and grow you into a vessel so that the next time something goes wrong, you will know how to effectively deal with it and have peace in the process. It will take both time and work, but I will be right by your side, supplying you with everything you need.

Yet you, Lord, are our Father. We are the clay,
you are the potter; we are all the work of your hand.

—Isaiah 64:8

JULY 30

You just got blindsided by someone you thought you had a good relationship with. The hurt and betrayal runs deep. The injustice and unfairness is rampant. You wonder what to do. You replay it in your mind over and over again, and you think hurtful things concerning the individual. It can consume you if you let it. But it feels good to you to go down that path and it relieves stress. But the truth is, it is only a temporary feeling. What you aren't seeing is the damage it is doing to your heart. It is turning your heart away from Me, and that is a dangerous place to be. I implore you to stop. Let Me fill you up with My goodness! I will show you what is going on in their lives to cause them to do what they did. Not that it is right, but it will help you to understand and to be able to show them compassion. They are broken, hurting and believing lies which can easily happen to you also. Turn your eyes to Me. Let Me fill you with My love. You can't change what happened or the other person, but you can change how it affects you! Let Me fill you with My peace even in the midst of this, and let Me give you My self-control. Take the better path of healing and restoration for yourself.

He was oppressed and afflicted, yet he did not open his mouth; he was led like a lamb to the
slaughter, and as a sheep before its shearers is silent, so he did not open his mouth.
—Isaiah 53:7

Even my close friend, someone I trusted, one who shared my bread, has turned against me.
—Psalm 41:9

You pray earnestly for something and are faithful to pray for it daily, believing that the prayer will be answered. You find out it isn't answered the way you thought or wanted it to be answered, and you are stunned and disappointed. You question whether you did something wrong in the way you prayed, or you wonder if I didn't hear you or even care. Questioning in itself isn't wrong, but what you do with these questions could be. My child, don't stay in this place of questioning. It serves no purpose. You didn't do anything wrong. Remember My thoughts are not your thoughts, nor My ways your ways. My timing is also different from yours. I see the whole picture, not just the small part that you are seeing. There are some things you won't be able to understand on your own. You have to trust that I know what I'm doing and draw from your relationship with Me and knowledge of My character. Some day you will understand My will, and you will see that your prayers were answered with your best interest in mind. Until then, I will give you comfort and My peace and patience as I continue to walk beside you.

How long, Lord, must I call for help, but you do not listen?
Or cry out to you, "Violence!" but you do not save?

—Habakkuk 1:2 NIV

Going a little farther, he fell with his face to the ground and prayed, "My Father,
if it is possible, may this cup be taken from me. Yet not as I will, but as you will."

—Matthew 26:39

AUGUST 1

$\mathcal{L}$ive from your fellowship with Me. Become so consumed with Me being a vital part of your life that you don't do anything or make any decisions without consulting with Me first. Realize I am part of you and I am your very life! Everything you are or do flows from My spirit within you. Receive from Me daily and live from My spirit and power being poured out through you. Do you have trouble with forgiveness? Turn to Me, connect and allow My forgiveness to flow out of you. Do you have trouble showing kindness? Step out of the way and allow My limitless amount of kindness to flow through you. Let My goodness flow out of you constantly. Please don't try to get ahead of Me or do anything in your own strength or wisdom. It really is that simple. Commune with Me constantly, step aside and allow Me to do the work, pouring out My goodness through you!

Very truly I tell you, whoever believes in me will do the works I have been doing, and they will do even greater things than these, because I am going to the Father.
—John 14:12

You are the light of the world. A town built on a hill cannot be hidden. Neither do people light a lamp and put it under a bowl. Instead they put it on its stand, and it gives light to everyone in the house. In the same way, let your light shine before others, that they may see your good deeds and glorify your Father in heaven.
—Matthew 5:14-16

AUGUST 2

$\mathcal{I}$ spoke everything into existence. I spoke and out of nothingness the world was formed along with all living creation! My words are powerful and miraculous. When I speak, it is because I have something to say. It is important for you to hear, respond and obey. I do nothing lightly; all is for an important purpose. My instruction to you is life-giving and life-changing. My warnings are for your protection. My nudges awaken you to the knowledge that the impossible is possible! My promises to you give you direction and hope. They are very real and require faith and trust on your part. I do everything out of My love for you. That is My motivation and purpose.

My word that goes out from my mouth: it will not return to me empty, but will accomplish what I desire and achieve the purpose for which I sent it.
—Isaiah 55:11

AUGUST 3

*Y*ou struggle with trusting in Me. You don't even want to admit it because you want to trust so badly. My dear one, I don't think less of you. I like that you are trying to do something about it and that it bothers you that you have trouble trusting. Let Me help you. Develop faith first as you learn more about Me in My Word and as you spend time with Me in My presence. Keep recalling all the times you felt My presence and My hand in a situation you were facing. Faith says that you know Me and believe. This takes some time and is a good foundation once you can do that. When you trust, you put faith into action. It's choosing to go from thinking that I can do what I promise you to declaring that I am doing for you what I promise you and that you will think and act accordingly. Keep getting to know Me better. Trust is built on that.

*"But blessed is the one who trusts in the Lord, whose confidence is in him.
They will be like a tree planted by the water that sends out its roots by the stream.
It does not fear when heat comes; its leaves are always green. It has no worries
in a year of drought and never fails to bear fruit."*

—Jeremiah 17:7-8

AUGUST 4

*D*on't feel bad when you don't know what you are doing. When you aren't relying on yourself, pride won't get in the way. Turn to Me immediately when you have no clue about what is happening or what to do, for I do know what is going on, and I see everything from beginning to end all at once. You can count on Me always knowing everything and how to best help you. When you totally surrender and rely on Me, you will be amazed at what will happen. Taking those first steps in faith can be a little scary, but as you continue to move forward with My lead, it is exhilarating and I will get the glory!

*Not that we are competent in ourselves to claim anything
for ourselves, but our competence comes from God.*

—2 Corinthians 3:5

No, in all these things we are more than conquerors through him who loved us.

—Romans 8:37

I use the sum total of your life to bring Me glory! Everything about your life I find a use for: your home life growing up, your experiences, challenges, heartbreaks and joys, even your creativity and idiosyncrasies! Nothing is wasted; everything about you happened for a reason and has a purpose. You are shaped and formed by these events as you allow Me to work in your life. You grow in maturity and character as you come to accept yourself the way you are and where you have come from. Your character and heart are what matter to Me. I want you to see and visualize your destiny and purpose and how special and worthy you really are to Me!

Do not be afraid, for I am with you; everyone who is called by my name,
whom I created for my glory, whom I formed and made.

—Isaiah 43:5a, 7

AUGUST 6

I am a God whom you can trust with your very life. I do not ever leave your side, no matter what you do, think, or say that is contrary to My will. In spite of your shortcomings, I continue to pursue you relentlessly, for that is My nature. I love you that much! I am there celebrating with you when you rejoice. In the midst of the storms, I am there supporting you, strengthening you and giving you direction. I walk with you as you go through day-to-day life, gently nudging you when you get off course. When you call out to Me, I answer and come to your aid. I am a God who is unchanging, unwavering and your biggest encourager!

Every good and perfect gift is from above, coming down from the
Father of the heavenly lights, who does not change like shifting shadows.

—James 1:17

*B*e careful what you are thinking. If your thoughts are positive and line up with My Word, they are pleasing to Me and are good thoughts to hold on to. If they are comforting, build you up, make you feel good about yourself, hold on to them. If you have any thoughts that make you feel bad, anxious, or stressed, or if these thoughts are ones you entertain over and over again and cause you grief, they are not from Me. Let go of those thoughts, immediately. Continue to reject these lies as they creep back into your mind. Know this My child. If I would correct you, I would not do it in a condemning way but in a way that gives you direction and loving support. When you are feeling bad inside and don't know why, recall what you are thinking about. If it is a thought that isn't from Me, dismiss it. Be careful what you allow in your mind. You will find you have more peace and contentment when you choose to only hold thoughts pleasing to Me.

Incline your ear and hear the words of the wise, and apply your mind to my knowledge.
—Proverbs 22:17 (NASB)

When my anxious thoughts multiply within me, your consolations delight my soul.
—Psalm 94:19 (NASB)

*G*uard your mind because what enters your mind can travel to your heart. Keep special protection around your heart, guarding it from the lies. Lies are not from Me. Your heart is where your passions, dreams and desires live. It is the part of you that connects with other people and with Me. It is important for you to guard it. You guard it by being careful of what you let into it. You guard it by being aware of your thoughts, and if they are not from Me, dismiss them immediately. If your heart is unhealthy, it can affect everything else. It can threaten your loved ones, friends, career and even your legacy! Your heart is under constant attack from hurts, disappointments and discouragements. Be very diligent about what you let into your heart.

Create in me a clean heart, O God, and renew a right spirit within me.
—Psalm 51:10 (ESV)

*The aim of our charge is love that issues from
a pure heart and a good conscience and a sincere faith.*
—1 Timothy 1:5 (ESV)

AUGUST 9

I have given you a tongue to express yourself. It is an instrument that can bring life to My people by speaking encouraging and kind words to them and by affirming them. It can also be used to destroy. When words come out that are mean-spirited, that causes Me pain and grieves Me so. When you are hurt or angered, you have an opportunity to let Me help you. I can empower you to refrain from saying what you're feeling at that precise moment. I can give you self-control. Will you choose the better way?

Whoever keeps his mouth and his tongue keeps himself out of trouble.
—Proverbs 21:23 (ESV)

But no human being can tame the tongue. It is a restless evil, full of deadly poison. With it we bless our Lord and Father, and with it we curse people who are made in the likeness of God. From the same mouth come blessing and cursing. My brothers, these things ought not to be so.
—James 3:8-10 (ESV)

AUGUST 10

I want you to pause for a moment to feel My very real presence. Become aware of My splendor all around you and in you. I have given you eyes to see what I am doing and a heart and mind to embrace and receive all I have for you. It is when you are connected to My loving presence that you begin to feel My peace flowing through you, My power surging in you, My strength and comfort sustaining you, and My love that empowers you and gives you your identity. In My presence, nothing else matters. All your struggles, worries and fears become small in the greatness of who I am. As you keep your eyes on Me, you find peace and even joy, knowing I am sovereign. Please, won't you consider giving Me total control of your life, trusting in Me and My love for you? I am a good God and a loving Father and I want so much for you to experience all I have for you, My child!

You make known to me the path of life; in your presence there is fullness of joy; at your right hand are pleasures forevermore.
—Psalm 16:11 (ESV)

AUGUST 11

*Y*ou may have experienced rejection in your life. It may have been from members of your family, a boss, spouse, friend, peer, or a church member. You feel worthless, unwanted and abandoned. It attacks the very person that you are. It destroys your self-esteem, your purpose and direction in life. It causes emotional wounds that, if not healed and released, will turn into spiritual wounds of unforgiveness, bitterness, envy, rejecting yourself, or even blaming Me! The enemy loves when this happens and wants you to keep holding on to these negative emotions. Don't do it. You can't change the other person or what happened, and many times the other person's actions were out of their own brokenness. But you can change yourself. I can help you. I want you to know I love you and accept you just the way you are. I see you as a person of great worth and of so much worth that My Son died for you. I want to see you be set free and believe in the person I created you to be! You don't need approval from man, only Me. Think about these truths, and embrace My love, acceptance and appreciation of you!

For my father and my mother have forsaken me, but the Lord will take me in.
—Psalm 27:10 (ESV)

AUGUST 12

*C*ome into My presence and spend time with Me. Come to Me and stand right here next to Me. I want to open the eyes of your heart so that you will see Me, so that when you look into My eyes, what you see is the depth of My love radiating from them. And as you look closer, you will see the tears in My eyes that show just how great that love is for you, My dear child. This is My heart poured out for you.

But because of his great love for us, God, who is rich in mercy, made us alive with
Christ even when we were dead in transgressions—it is by grace you have been saved.
—Ephesians 2:4-5

Greater love has no one than this: to lay down one's life for one's friends.
—John 15:13

AUGUST 13

*D*o you ever feel that I have rejected you? You may think this because of something you did or because you don't feel worthy enough. I want you to know that this thought is a lie you are believing. I would never reject you because it is not in My nature to reject you. I love you with an unconditional love. There is nothing you could do that would cause Me to want to reject you. When you have these thoughts, know that they are not from Me but are lies from the enemy who is trying to kill, steal and destroy. When you have these thoughts, do not entertain them. Dismiss them immediately! At the same time that you empty your mind of these thoughts, fill your mind with My truth. I will never leave you or forsake you, for you are My child, whom I dearly love!

For you are a people holy to the Lord your God. Out of all the peoples
on the face of the earth, the Lord has chosen you to be his treasured possession.
—Deuteronomy 14:2

What, then, shall we say in response to these things? If God is for us, who can be against us?
—Romans 8:31

AUGUST 14

*D*o you know how I see you? I see you as a person of beauty and of great worth. You have been redeemed and restored. I see righteousness and purity, for you were cleansed with the blood of Jesus since you are a believer. I know you don't always feel righteous and pure, for I know you still struggle with repeating the same sins even when you try not to and you repeatedly repent. Never go by your feelings. I have cleansed you. Nothing has to get in the way of what I have done for you. Let go of the weight and step into who you are in Me. You are equipped with everything you need for victory. Step into the truth of who you are!

But now apart from the law the righteousness of God has been made known,
to which the Law and the Prophets testify. This righteousness is given through faith
in Jesus Christ to all who believe. There is no difference between Jew and Gentile,
for all have sinned and fall short of the glory of God.
—Romans 3:21-23

AUGUST 15

*W*hat is your attitude when you come to church on a Sunday morning? Are you stressed and frazzled about things going on in your life or about getting everyone out the door on time? Are you coming because that is what you do when you're a Christian? Once inside, are you just singing meaningless words and going through the motions but feeling empty or even dead inside? Oh, My child, let Me show you a better way! Awaken to the reality that you really are meeting Me face-to-face! You may not see it with your earthly eyes, but that is what is happening in My eyes! Come with a freshness of awe and wonder and excitement, anticipating an encounter with Me! Sing the songs as if singing the words directly to Me. Pray as if I am right there next to you. Praise Me with such gratitude that tears come to your eyes. It's a different mindset. I want you to begin to realize My presence is right there in front of you! Seek the wonder in this!

Praise the Lord. Praise God in his sanctuary; praise him in his mighty heavens.
Praise him for his acts of power; praise him for his surpassing greatness.
—Psalm 150:1-2

A cheerful heart is good medicine, but a crushed spirit dries up the bones.
—Proverbs 17:22

AUGUST 16

*L*ook for My goodness throughout your day in everything you do and experience. There are no coincidences. I put people in your path to give you words that you need to hear. The song you are listening to, which all of a sudden speaks My truth to you, is from Me. When you find unexpected money or provision, see a brilliant sunrise or sunset, or are spared from an accident that there's no way you should have avoided, these things are all from Me. My goodness reveals My nature. I am the foundation of goodness and everything that is good. It is all generated from Me, for I didn't obtain it from any other source. Purposefully look for My goodness and you will be amazed at how many times you will find it!

Taste and see that the Lord is good; blessed is the one who takes refuge in him.
—Psalm 34:8

You are good, and what you do is good; teach me your decrees.
—Psalm 119:68

AUGUST 17

*S*erve Me and earnestly seek truth. Stand firm on My truths and on My promises to you. Do not waiver or second guess yourself. Do not be concerned with what people think about you. That is just the enemy trying to influence you. I don't want you to miss out on My best by succumbing to the world's ways. I will give you the strength you need when you are challenged. Be bold in My boldness when speaking My truth to others, but remember to do so with My love.

So then, brothers and sisters, stand firm and hold fast to the
teachings we passed on to you, whether by word of mouth or by letter.
—2 Thessalonians 2:15

Fear of man will prove to be a snare, but whoever trusts in the Lord is kept safe.
—Proverbs 29:25

AUGUST 18

I want to caution you not to get prideful because of what you know or studied or by what you have done for years. Knowledge puffs up, but love builds up. It's My joy to give revelation to My people. I hide it from those who will feel self-important in their own experiences and rely on themselves. Your position or title is not what I look at, for I look at your heart, which cannot be hidden from Me. Give Me your humbled heart and I will do great things through you and for My kingdom!

Do nothing out of selfish ambition or vain conceit. Rather, in humility value others above
yourselves, not looking to your own interests but each of you to the interests of the others.
—Philippians 2:3-4

But he gives us more grace. That is why Scripture says:
"God opposes the proud but shows favor to the humble."
—James 4:6

AUGUST 19

*W*hen a situation comes up and you know everyone else is siding with the world's way, but you know that is not My way, what are you going to do? You have an important choice to make. I want you to make a faith decision and choose Me, which may put you in the minority. Look at My daughter, Rahab, an unlikely candidate who ended up in the Hall of Faith in the Bible. She didn't perish with all the rest who didn't believe because she stepped out in faith and protected the "enemy" spies. She focused on My mission, knew these spies were from Me and risked everything, including her very life, to hide them from harm. Because of her wise choice, she and her family's lives were spared and she was blessed. I give you that same courage and strength if you step out in faith and choose to follow Me.

By faith the prostitute Rahab, because she welcomed the spies,
was not killed with those who were disobedient.

—Hebrews 11:31

AUGUST 20

*Y*ou look at your life or the life of someone you care about deeply and see the shambles it is in. You see the wrong things that you've done like addictions, blatant sins, bad choices, wrong company, or wrong thinking, and this cycle keeps repeating itself. It doesn't have to stay this way. My Son paid the price for a redeemed life. Come to Me, My child. Choose to repent, ask for forgiveness and turn away from these sins. I will give you My strength and all you need to repent if you just make the choice. A redeemed life includes having eternal life with Me, forgiveness of your sins, an awesome relationship with Me, adoption into My family and resting in My peace. It is a totally transformed life with a new purpose. It doesn't get better than that. My Son did it for you, so won't you receive this new life?

For all have sinned and fall short of the glory of God, and all are
justified freely by his grace through the redemption that came by Christ Jesus.
—Romans 3:23-24

While we wait for the blessed hope—the appearing of the glory of our great God
and Savior, Jesus Christ, who gave himself for us to redeem us from all wickedness
and to purify for himself a people that are his very own, eager to do what is good.
—Titus 2:13-14

AUGUST 21

$\mathcal{M}$y Word is pure and true. It is always valid and stands the test of time. It applies to every situation you face and gives you guidance and direction for living. It is not always easy to understand, but press in for a deeper grasp. Ask Me to give you insight and how to apply My Word to your life. Keep persevering and being persistent. The more you read, attend Bible studies and spend time with Me, the clearer it becomes. Store My words in your heart, so you can recall them when needed. I ask for you to fear Me, but it is a different kind of fear than what you think. It is having a reverent trust in Me, who I am and what I say in My Word, which then results in a sincere obedience coming from your heart. As you continue to pursue My Word, it will become a treasure to you, for you will realize just how priceless it is!

My son, if you accept my words and store up my commands within you, turning your ear to wisdom and applying your heart to understanding— indeed, if you call out for insight and cry aloud for understanding, and if you look for it as for silver and search for it as for hidden treasure, then you will understand the fear of the Lord and find the knowledge of God. For the Lord gives wisdom; from his mouth come knowledge and understanding.
—Proverbs 2:1-6

AUGUST 22

$\mathcal{C}$ome to Me as a child. Lay down your fears, your doubts and your unbeliefs. Tear down the wall that keeps part of Me out because you're not ready to give up control of your life. You struggle with these feelings and hold on to these things, yet I pursue you without any condemnation. I want you to let go of everything holding you back and put your trust in Me for every aspect of your life. I am grieved because I see what is lacking in your life, and I can fill it with My power and love. You don't have to live like this ever again. Please, come to Me with a childlike faith and embrace My peace and joy.

Truly I tell you, anyone who will not receive the kingdom of God like a little child will never enter it.
—Mark 10:15

Though you have not seen him, you love him; and even though you do not see him now, you believe in him and are filled with an inexpressible and glorious joy, for you are receiving the end result of your faith, the salvation of your souls.
—1 Peter 1:8-9

$\mathcal{Y}$ou are dealing with an ongoing difficult situation. Each day you are connecting to Me. The road isn't always easy and there are delays and obstacles, but everything continues to work out. But now there is a major setback and you are discouraged. You wonder, "Will this ever end? Will I ever be back on my feet?" Pause and reconnect to Me. Is anything really different? Am I not the same God who comforts, protects, provides and guides? Am I not the one who said, "Trust in Me with all your heart and do not lean on your own understanding. In all your ways acknowledge Me and I will direct your paths?" Am I not the one who said, "I know the plans I have for you, plans to prosper you and not to harm you, plans to give you hope and a future?" Am I not the one who said, "Take up My yoke upon you, and learn from Me, for I am gentle and humble in heart, and you will find rest for your souls?" Am I not the one who said, "Do not be anxious about anything, but in every situation, by prayer and petition, with thanksgiving, present your requests to Me?" Have I not commanded you, "Be strong and courageous. Do not be afraid; do not be discouraged, for I will be with you wherever you go?" Stay focused on My promises to you and persevere through the storm.

Not only so, but we also glory in our sufferings, because we know that suffering produces perseverance; perseverance, character; and character, hope. And hope does not put us to shame, because God's love has been poured out into our hearts through the Holy Spirit, who has been given to us. —Romans 5:3-5

Look to the Lord and his strength; seek his face always. —1 Chronicles 16:11

$\mathcal{W}$hat do you do when you wake up tired and grumpy, nothing seems to be going right about your day and negative thoughts fill your mind? You have a choice to make. You can stay on that path by believing the lies and fueling the lies with more negative thoughts, or you can pause, refocus and choose a better way which is My way! Choose to purposefully make these declarations to yourself. "Today is a great day. I choose to let go of all negative thoughts. I choose to find joy in this day. I choose to find Your goodness, Lord. I have been given everything I need for life and godliness." Repeat these declarations as often as needed. Watch how your outlook will change!

Do everything without grumbling or arguing. —Philippians 2:14

I remain confident of this: I will see the goodness of the Lord in the land of the living. —Psalm 27:13

AUGUST 25

*H*ow many times are you influenced by negative things others say or think about you? What do you do when they say that you can't do something or that you aren't good enough? You may repeatedly play these words over and over again in your mind. Often times whatever you fix your mind on, you become. These people may not even be aware of the damage they are causing with their careless and thoughtless remarks. These are lies, My child. They have no idea of your potential. They don't see what I see. They didn't create you or see who you really are and what you will become, but I do! Focus on what is true, which are My Word and My promises to you. These will unlock all you've been made to do and be. Your potential is already here. Become it!

However, as it is written: "What no eye has seen, what no ear has heard, and what no human mind has conceived, these are the things God has prepared for those who love him."
—1 Corinthians 2:9

I pray that the eyes of your heart may be enlightened in order that you may know the hope to which he has called you, the riches of his glorious inheritance in his holy people.
—Ephesians 1:18

AUGUST 26

I gladly receive all kinds of prayers. They don't have to be flowery or scholarly, but I value prayers that come straight from your heart. Let Me show you some different ways to pray. Make it a point to worship Me throughout your prayer time. Pray believing, not pleading. Pray with thanksgiving and declare My truths rather than asking for what is already done. Address the problem and, in My Son's name, command it to leave rather than praying about the issue. You have that power and authority if you know and believe in Me. Don't spend time dwelling on the enemy and his schemes, but focus on My power and protection already in place to release blessings. Focus on My goodness and that the victory is already there.

This is the confidence we have in approaching God: that if we ask anything according to his will, he hears us.
—1 John 5:14

Then you will call on me and come and pray to me, and I will listen to you.
—Jeremiah 29:12

AUGUST 27

*W*hen you are wounded by others, it is hard to reconcile what happened because you have no control over another, only over yourself. You are sorry the situation happened and mourn the loss. Take some time, My child. Surrender to My ways and go through the process with Me right by your side. Choose to draw your strength from Me to forgive and to let go of all bitterness, anger and blame. Give yourself time to rest, regroup and recover with the skills you learn through this process. Eventually you will be restored and the healing will be completed.

And the God of all grace, who called you to his eternal glory in Christ, after you have suffered a little while, will himself restore you and make you strong, firm and steadfast.
—1 Peter 5:10

The Lord is close to the brokenhearted and saves those who are crushed in spirit.
—Psalm 34:18 NIV

AUGUST 28

*W*hen you look at people, what do you see? Do you judge them, even subconsciously, by their appearance or by what they say or do? Please stop this habit, for it serves no purpose. Instead, begin to look at their potential. Start looking at them the way I see them. See their destiny and My plans for them. They are the same plans as I have for you: plans to prosper and not to harm you, plans to give you hope and a future. Remember, I can transform someone's life in a moment. I see the possibilities in a person's failures. See what I see in people and start looking at them that way. Watch how things will change in the way they interact and respond to you.

For God gave us a spirit not of fear but of power and love and self-control.
—2 Timothy 1:7 (ESV)

"For I know the plans I have for you," declares the Lord, "plans to prosper you and not to harm you, plans to give you hope and a future."
—Jeremiah 29:11

*A*s you walk side-by-side with Me, you will attract people to you—not so much by outward appearance which is fleeting but by your inward appearance. They see your heart which is aligned with My heart. Because you live your life for Me, they see a difference that they are drawn to and also want to have. Become aware of the possibility that people watch how you respond to situations, how you handle yourself and what you say. I'm not saying this to make you feel intimidated, but for you to become aware that this is happening and that your life is being used for My glory. People also learn from your mistakes and how you handle them. They notice if you say you're sorry and ask for forgiveness without placing blame on someone else. Allow Me to guide you in every situation you face as you continue to be My ambassador. You may be the only Bible that some people experience!

Whoever claims to live in him must live as Jesus did.

—1 John 2:6

To this you were called, because Christ suffered for you,
leaving you an example, that you should follow in his steps.

—1 Peter 2:21

---

*W*hen you are in the midst of a crisis or find yourself in an overwhelming situation, what thoughts go through your mind? See if any thoughts are contradictory to My Truth, who I am to you and the promises I have made to you. If they are, choose to release them immediately. Turn your thoughts back to Me. You may feel unsure, insecure, offended, or many other things, but these feelings are not coming from Me and are not true. Step into the reality of My Truth, rather than remain in the reality of your circumstance.

I can do all this through him who gives me strength. And my God will
meet all your needs according to the riches of his glory in Christ Jesus.
—Philippians 4:13,19

Through these he has given us his very great and precious promises,
so that through them you may participate in the divine nature, having
escaped the corruption in the world caused by evil desires.

—2 Peter 1:4

$\mathcal{F}$rom time to time you are concerned about end times. You hear the unbeliev-able news of more atrocities, mass destruction and catastrophes. It is overwhelming at times and also very frightening. You wonder what's next and when it will involve your loved ones or how bad will it get. Lies start to creep in, and you entertain them. My child, don't allow your thoughts to center on any of this. Choose to refocus on Me and prepare for what is to come. Repent and turn from your sinful and prideful ways and seek My ways. Come to know Me as your Savior and Lord. Read what My Word says about the end times. It is all written down so there won't be any surprises. My Son's death, burial and resurrection have been completed for your eternal reward because I care about you that much. Once this preparation is in place, you will find strength and peace in Me, knowing I am in control. It won't always be easy, but I am there every step with you. Remember that I am bigger than any of this, that I am sovereign and that you already know the ending!

For God so loved the world that he gave his one and only Son,
that whoever believes in him shall not perish but have eternal life. —John 3:16

I will show wonders in the heavens and on the earth, blood and fire and billows of smoke.
The sun will be turned to darkness and the moon to blood before the coming of the great and
dreadful day of the Lord. And everyone who calls on the name of the Lord will be saved.
—Joel 2:30-32a

SEPTEMBER 1

*S*ometimes you are hard on yourself. You are hungry and thirsty for more of Me, you're on fire for Me and you're in a hurry to grow and to be used mightily by Me. I love your passion and your thirst. It gives Me great joy. But, please don't get ahead of Me. Follow My lead and timing. Please don't despise small beginnings. You also are critical of yourself when you think you have blown it, reacted poorly to a situation, or done something you know wasn't pleasing to Me. Please don't be ashamed of training wheels or wrecks as you learn to grow. I see the progress you are making, not the setbacks. Focus on what I see.

Blessed are those who hunger and thirst for righteousness, for they will be filled.
—Matthew 5:6

Do not despise these small beginnings, for the Lord rejoices to see the work begin.
—Zechariah 4:10a (NLT)

SEPTEMBER 2

*Y*ou fear many things and sometimes aren't even aware of it. If you will peel off the layers of things holding you back, you will see the root is fear. Fear and faith cannot live in your heart at the same time, for fear frequently blinds your eyes to My presence. Courage and faith are the opposites of fear, and that is what I want you to have. Stop running from the thing you fear and face it with all of your faith in Me. That is courage and faith in action. Intimacy with Me cultivates faith. When you spend time with Me, you get to know My nature and character and My perfect plans and purposes for you. Your courage and faith stem from your confidence in Me and My promises to you. Perfect love casts out fear. Fear is not from Me but from the enemy. I am love perfected and I am all powerful. So take courage and find your faith and strength in Me.

Be on your guard; stand firm in the faith; be courageous; be strong.
—1 Corinthians 16:13

Be strong and courageous. Do not be afraid or terrified because of them,
for the Lord your God goes with you; he will never leave you nor forsake you.
—Deuteronomy 31:6

SEPTEMBER 3

*Y*ou have a very strong work ethic. You have each day planned out with exactly what you are going to accomplish. You feel good getting it all done and it gives you satisfaction. When things get in the way of your plans or your body is saying that you need a break, you feel guilty because you feel that you're not getting anything accomplished. Even when you rest or take a break, you have trouble relaxing because you feel as if you're not doing anything. These are lies you are believing. My child, I want you to step back a moment and see things from My perspective. I place great importance on rest and set the example in Genesis. Rest will begin to come naturally to you when you start to trust that I will take care of things for you and that when you take a day off, it is a positive thing and pleasing to Me. Please let go of controlling your life, work, family—of controlling everything. Turn the control back to Me in faith, and that will give you the freedom to relax. Consciously choose to let go of the lies and control and rest in Me.

Six days you shall labor, but on the seventh day you shall rest;
even during the plowing season and harvest you must rest.
—Exodus 34:21

SEPTEMBER 4

*O*nce in a while, you think about where will you go when you die. You know in your mind that you are a Christian and that you will spend eternity in heaven. But if you are totally honest with yourself, there's a gnawing feeling in your heart that you don't really know for certain. Oh, My child, I want you to know for sure. My Son's death, burial and resurrection conquered sin and death. If you accept Jesus Christ as your Savior, you receive eternal life as a free gift. Read the passages in My Word that talk about eternal life, and write them on your heart. Spend time with Me, getting to know Me through a personal relationship. Do not entertain any lies that question My Word or where you will spend eternity. Rest in My Word and My assurance to you.

They replied, "Believe in the Lord Jesus, and you will be saved—you and your household."
—Acts 16:31

And if I go and prepare a place for you, I will come back and take you
to be with me that you also may be where I am.
—John 14:3

SEPTEMBER 5

*M*y Word is filled with truth. This truth grounds you. It is the firm foundation that you can claim as real and unchanging. I give you a standard that you can use to constantly test your thought life. If your thoughts don't line up with My Word and My Truth, you then have the boldness and confidence to dismiss them as lies and purposefully not entertain them again. In their place, fill your mind with My Truth. You will find such freedom in this.

Then you will know the truth, and the truth will set you free. —John 8:32

Sanctify them by the truth; your word is truth. —John 17:17

SEPTEMBER 6

*Y*ou look back at your life and the choices you made and feel regret, sadness and guilt. You feel unworthy and ashamed because of these decisions. These thoughts constantly come back to you and each time you entertain them, they intensify your negative feelings. My child, please stop doing this to yourself. I see your pain and it grieves My heart because I love you so much. I want you to tell Me what you did and confess it as sin. Then repent by turning your back to it, turn to Me instead, and desire to do things that are pleasing to Me. Your sins are forgiven when you confess and repent and I see them no more. What I see is a repentant heart, a heart that wants to live for Me. I see the wonderful child I created you to be with an equally wonderful purpose and destiny ahead of you! Please begin to see yourself as I see you. Recall in the Bible how King David committed adultery and murder, but then repented and how I called him a man after My own heart. Ask Me for wisdom and guidance in your decisions and choices and I will gladly help you. Learn from past mistakes and then choose to let them go. Your past does not define who you are or how I see you. This is a new day! I will equip and guide your path if you allow Me to. You may still stumble, but keep holding My hand because I'm not letting go of you. Walk with Me, My child, and see yourself the way I see you.

After removing Saul, he made David their king. God testified concerning him: 'I have found David son of Jesse, a man after my own heart; he will do everything I want him to do.'
—Acts 13:22

In him we have redemption through his blood, the forgiveness of sins, in accordance with the riches of God's grace.
—Ephesians 1:7

SEPTEMBER 7

*S*ometimes things don't always work out as planned. You found out you have to postpone retirement, or can't quit the job that you dislike, or can't move just yet to a nicer place. You suddenly are laid up with an unexpected injury, or illness that could take months or years until you are back to normal. Any number of things can happen to postpone your plans and what you were looking forward to. You begin to dwell on what you don't have and having to wait for months or years seems daunting. As a result you begin to feel trapped, hopeless and depressed. You hate feeling this way. My child, it doesn't have to be like this. Yes, there are things you can't change, but you can still live life filled with My joy and peace. Please stop dwelling on what you don't have and what happened in your life to change things. It does no good and only intensifies the negative feelings you have. Instead, turn to Me and let Me fill you up with peace and contentment. Feel My presence, giving you hope and courage to continue on in My strength. Feel My power constantly flowing through you. Look for the blessings that you do have and be thankful for them. Take one day at a time and look for the goodness in the day. Even while living with unmet desires, you can have My peace because that is why My Son died. Please change what your thoughts are focused on and redirect them to what I am doing in and through you. Abiding in My peace is so much better.

Keep your lives free from the love of money and be content with what you have, because God has said, "Never will I leave you; never will I forsake you."
—Hebrews 13:5

SEPTEMBER 8

*T*hings happen in your life that you weren't expecting and that cause tremendous stress and discomfort. You're shocked when it happens, feel powerless and have no idea how to find a solution. My child, I use times like this to get your attention and to show you My glory by what I will do for you. I want you to take the focus off what you can do and focus on what I am doing through you to help resolve things. Please, come to Me and give Me your burden. I am always here for you; I love you that much.

Give your entire attention to what God is doing right now, and don't get worked up about what may or may not happen tomorrow. God will help you deal with whatever hard things come up when the time comes. —Matthew 6:34 (MSG)

*Y*ou are surrounded every day by people who try your patience, who offend you, and who are difficult to deal with. You don't want to judge them, but you end up doing so anyway. Please remember that they are hurting and you could have easily been one of them if you weren't following Me. Remember you can't judge and love them at the same time, so choose to love them with My love. Treat them not as they treat you but in the way I treat you. When they are at their lowest point go to them and demonstrate My love. It can be life-changing for both of you. I encourage you not to expect anything in return and not to give up on them. May your motive be to demonstrate My love and compassion, knowing each hurting person has a heart and soul. You can be a part of changing someone's life in a moment and when they may need it most.

Fools show their annoyance at once, but the prudent overlook an insult.
—Proverbs 12:16

It is my prayer that your love may abound more and more, with knowledge and all discernment.
—Philippians 1:9 (ESV)

SEPTEMBER 10

I know you love Me, but sometimes if you are being honest with yourself, you aren't so sure if you trust Me. You struggle with knowing My will and wanting to follow it but wanting to do it your own way. You're not frightened by My love for you, but you are scared of what I may take from you or what I'll ask you to do. I don't say that to be condemning but to open your eyes to the reality. My child, please know that I love you. I would never intentionally hurt you or make you do something on a whim. Out of My love for you, I may ask you to do things that will cause you to be stretched and build your character for your own benefit. You will learn skills that will help you the next time a situation comes up that causes distress so that you can find peace in the midst of it. I walk with you constantly, guiding and equipping you when I ask you to do something. Please trust in Me and know I want the best for you!

Those who know your name trust in you, for you, Lord, have never forsaken those who seek you.
—Psalm 9:10

Commit your way to the Lord; trust in him, and he will act. He will bring forth your righteousness as the light, and your justice as the noonday.
—Psalm 37:5-6 (ESV)

SEPTEMBER 11

I have given you a free will for a reason. I want you to experience My love and to give and receive love. But love is a choice, and I want you to choose it on your own, not because I programed you to. I want you to come to Me because you want to, not because I made you come. I want a relationship with you more than you can imagine. But I will not force you to spend time with Me. I will love you regardless and with the same intensity because that is My nature. You have a free will, but My desire is that you make choices that are pleasing to Me and to love as I love.

Here I am! I stand at the door and knock. If anyone hears my voice
and opens the door, I will come in and eat with that person, and they with me.
—Revelation 3:20

In their hearts humans plan their course, but the Lord establishes their steps.
—Proverbs 16:9

SEPTEMBER 12

*Y*ou see the unfairness of life. Bad things happening to good people and good things happening to people who don't follow Me. You have trouble understanding this. You question why trials happen to you because you are a Christian following My ways, doing everything right, and you think it is unfair. This is a lie you are believing that Christians are exempt from bad things happening to them. I am not the creator of evil. This is the result of the fallen nature of man. Because of the cross, I give you eternal life in the future and abundant life for now. I am right by your side, providing what is needed to see you through these difficult times with peace, strength and even joy. Pursue Me and connect to My abundant life which you can have even as you experience unfairness and trials.

Cast your cares on the Lord and he will sustain you; he will never let the righteous be shaken.
—Psalm 55:22

*T*here will be pain, evil and suffering in this world. But please understand; I did not cause those things. I created the Garden of Eden, which was My perfect paradise and was My intention for this world that you live in. Sin is present as a direct result of the fallen nature of man. I do promise to cause good to emerge from the evil and suffering if you are committed to Me. Sometimes you will see the good soon afterwards but sometimes not in your lifetime. Look at the greatest example of this, at how the horrific death of My Son could be turned into something good: the opening of Heaven, forgiveness of sins and eternal and abundant life! I can turn evil into something positive which will draw you closer to Me, shape and define your character and draw others to Me. Look for the good in every situation.

God saw all that he had made, and it was very good.
And there was evening, and there was morning—the sixth day.
—Genesis 1:3

We know that God causes all things to work together for good
to those who love God, to those who are called according to His purpose.
—Romans 8:28 (NASB)

I want you to give thanks in all circumstances. Rejoice even when there doesn't seem as if there is anything to rejoice about. I know it is not always easy for you to do this. You question how you can rejoice when you are depressed, seriously ill, under financial pressure, or in any number of serious situations. But that doesn't change the command. When you choose to rejoice, it gets My attention and pleases Me. It shows Me a surrendered heart. I want you to rejoice because your focus is on Me and what I am doing in your life, rather than on the situation you face. It is an attitude I want you to cultivate and live by. You are redirecting your focus. As you rejoice, you are realizing I am your comforter, provider, healer, strength, wisdom and everything you need. You are rejoicing in Me and not your circumstance. Please, follow My command; it really does make a difference!

Rejoice in the Lord always. I will say it again: Rejoice!   —Philippians 4:4

Rejoice always, pray continually, give thanks in all circumstances;
for this is God's will for you in Christ Jesus.   —1 Thessalonians 5:16-18

SEPTEMBER 15

*T*here will come a day when suffering will cease. Every person will be held accountable and I will judge evil. That is My promise to you in My Word. You sometimes wonder why I'm not doing it now. If I have the power to wipe out all pain, evil and suffering, why am I waiting so long to act? I have a purpose in all things. I see the entire picture from beginning to end, not just one piece. My desire is that all mankind will repent and come to Me. I don't want to lose anyone to eternal fire. I want all to put their trust in Me and spend eternity with Me. My love for all mankind is that great. Help Me by sharing the Good News with all you know. Love like I love, not wanting anyone to perish.

The Lord is not slow in keeping his promise, as some understand slowness. Instead he is patient with you, not wanting anyone to perish, but everyone to come to repentance.
—2 Peter 3:9

For I consider that the sufferings of this present time are not worth comparing with the glory that is to be revealed to us.
—Romans 8:18 (ESV)

SEPTEMBER 16

*I*n times of suffering and distress, you have a choice. You can choose to turn angry and bitter and dwell on negative thoughts, or you can turn to Me for courage, strength, peace and hope. All suffering can be an opportunity for good to be realized. I give you peace and strength to deal with what you are going through now, and courage and hope to deal with your future. My Son dealt with every kind of suffering and understands how you feel. Pain and suffering don't have to define you or have the last word. Won't you choose the better way?

Not only so, but we also glory in our sufferings, because we know that suffering produces perseverance; perseverance, character; and character, hope. And hope does not put us to shame, because God's love has been poured out into our hearts through the Holy Spirit, who has been given to us.
—Romans 5:3-5

SEPTEMBER 17

*Y*ou read and memorize familiar Scriptures like the following: "Rejoice in the Lord always, again I say rejoice"; "Be Still and know that I am God"; "Perfect love casts out fear". You think to yourself that they sound great and probably are very meaningful, but truthfully, you just don't understand them let alone know how to apply them to your life. You feel ashamed and stupid. Please don't feel that way. Those are lies you are believing. The more you grow in spiritual maturity, read My Word and spend time with Me; the more you will understand it. Ask Me for help and insight and to open your mind so you can better understand and apply My Word to your life. Read commentaries from teachers I have equipped and attend Bible studies. Use this information to go back to My Word for clarification, but guard against changing My Word to suit your or other's interpretations or opinions. Please don't get discouraged because that is what the enemy wants you to do. Keep reading and know I am here helping you understand.

Then Philip ran up to the chariot and heard the man reading Isaiah the prophet. "Do you understand what you are reading?" Philip asked. "How can I," he said, "unless someone explains it to me?" Then Philip began with that very passage of Scripture and told him the good news about Jesus.
—Acts 8:30-31 & 35

SEPTEMBER 18

*W*hat I would like most of all from you is a closer relationship. I would like that more than all the things you do for Me or for others. I want your focus to be on getting to know Me better so that you will be able to trust My words and promises to you when you are going through trials. It will make your life so much easier and lighten your load. I don't need anything from you. You don't have to do anything for Me. I will love you regardless and that will never change. My love isn't dependent on what you do. I never want to make you feel guilty, and I never do anything with strings attached. That is not in My nature. If you do something that is not pleasing to Me, I will let you know in a way that is not condemning, and I will show you a better way so that it benefits you. If you decide to do something for Me though, you will be blessed. It is out of a love relationship with Me that you will want to do things pleasing to Me because it will make you feel good inside. I love you, My child; come closer!

Whoever does not love does not know God, because God is love.
—1 John 4:8

*W*hen you are going through a storm, remember that I am your source of refuge, a mighty fortress that cannot be shaken. I am right by your side in times of trouble, supporting you, sustaining you and lifting you up. Even if the end is nowhere in sight, I want you to persevere and depend on Me. Do not be afraid or give up. Claim My promises and stand on them. My kingdom is unshakable and it will not fail. Place your faith in My words. Remember, My child, I am right by your side, encouraging you and giving you what you need to see you through.

*Therefore, since we are receiving a kingdom that cannot be shaken,
let us be thankful, and so worship God acceptably with reverence and awe.*
—Hebrews 12:28

*The Lord is my rock, my fortress and my deliverer; my God is my rock,
in whom I take refuge, my shield and the horn of my salvation, my stronghold.*
—Psalm 18:2

SEPTEMBER 20

*Y*ou may have faithfully gone to church your whole life and have done many good things. You say you know Me, but if you are honest with yourself, you may find Me to be a distant, intimidating God. You choose to keep Me at bay and you may not even be aware that you are doing this. You just want to feel like a good Christian, live a normal life and then go to heaven. You want to do this, but all the while not get too close to Me, where you would feel pressured or frightened. Those are lies you are believing. My child, you feel this way because you just know of Me; you really don't know who I am or know My character and nature. I encourage you to get to know Me. Spend time with Me by telling Me about your day, just like you would with someone else you enjoy spending time with. Learn about Me in My word. Talk with others who know and love Me or go to a Bible study. Desire getting to know Me, not just knowing of Me, for it really will make a difference in your life.

*Thus says the Lord: "Let not the wise man boast in his wisdom, let not the mighty man
boast in his might, let not the rich man boast in his riches, but let him who boasts boast
in this, that he understands and knows me, that I am the Lord who practices steadfast love,
justice, and righteousness in the earth. For in these things I delight, declares the Lord."*
—Jeremiah 9:23-24 (ESV)

𝒞ome into My presence, standing face to face with Me in total intimacy, where nothing else matters but your worship of Me. Everything else in life falls away. May your heart be undone and opened to all I have for you. Commit your life into My hands, where you freely give Me all that you are. Here you are able to trust Me with confidence because you know Me so well. You know My nature and character and who I am to you. Your love and service to Me will flow out of this intimate relationship that we have. Continue to press in for more and you will be blessed!

You, God, are my God, earnestly I seek you; I thirst for you, my whole being longs for you, in a dry and parched land where there is no water. I have seen you in the sanctuary and beheld your power and your glory. Because your love is better than life, my lips will glorify you.
—Psalm 63:1-3

𝒴ou hear the word "repent" and it brings up negative thoughts and feelings. The only way you were presented with the concept of repentance was in a fire and brimstone kind of way, void of love, and full of fear and guilt. Please, let Me show you a different way. I do want you to repent, but it's because I love and care about you and don't want to see you suffer the consequences of continuing to choose something harmful to you and displeasing to Me. When you repent, choose to turn your back on the sin and turn towards Me. When you make that choice, it allows Me to help you by giving you self-control and everything you need to follow through. I give you strength when you falter and encourage you to continue. I am there every step of the way, helping you stay on the right path. I do this because I love you that much.

If we confess our sins, he is faithful and just and will forgive us our sins and purify us from all unrighteousness. —1 John 1:9

Repent, then, and turn to God, so that your sins may be wiped out, that times of refreshing may come from the Lord. —Acts 3:19

SEPTEMBER 23

There are constant changes in your life. You are used to doing something a certain way when suddenly you need to do it differently, and it's a hardship. Health issues arise, loved ones die, children leave home and friendships come and go. Our nation and world situations change. You find some of the changes difficult, and you get frustrated and wonder if anything will ever stay the same. In all these changes there is one constant; I do not change. I am the same yesterday, today and tomorrow. My Word doesn't change either. My promises to you are forever. I will never leave your side. These are truths that won't be changed. You can count on them.

There is a time for everything, and a season for every activity under the heavens.
—Ecclesiastes 3:1

Jesus Christ is the same yesterday and today and forever.
—Hebrews 13:8

SEPTEMBER 24

There are some things in your life that you have to do but would rather not do. Sometimes you accomplish them grudgingly, do a poor job, or completely omit doing them. Doing it this way, the focus is on yourself and how much you don't want to do the task. Since these jobs are part of your life, it will help you if you change your focus and your thinking. Try working at them as an expression of My love. Think of it as a way to express My love to others. Take your focus off what you don't enjoy to find the positives and the opportunities to shine and be at your best! The way you do your work reflects on the way you see the calling on your life. Work for Me, not people or yourself; and do everything as if you are doing it unto Me.

And whatever you do, whether in word or deed, do it all in the name
of the Lord Jesus, giving thanks to God the Father through him.
—Colossians 3:17

Whatever you do, work at it with all your heart, as working for the Lord,
not for human masters, since you know that you will receive an inheritance
from the Lord as a reward. It is the Lord Christ you are serving.
—Colossians 3:23-24

SEPTEMBER 25

*Y*ou or someone you know may be feeling dirty, ashamed, or worthless over something that you did or was done to you. As a result, you feel unworthy and unclean to come to Me, so you back away and hold your distance. These are lies you are believing. Shame holds you to your past, steals your joy, makes you settle for less than you deserve, and won't let you receive My love. My child, I grieve for you! I long to heal your wounds, take away your pain and set you free. If you haven't already done so, tell Me about what you did or what was done to you. Choose to turn away from that sin or thought and ask for forgiveness. My forgiveness is real, and I see your sin no more. Choose to see yourself as I see you and stop thinking about your past. If something was done to you, it was not your fault. Choose to let go of that lie. I will judge the person Myself, but I want you to choose to forgive them for your sake. My child, I see you as having great worth, not for what you did but because of how I created you and what My Son did for you. You are My masterpiece and I don't make mistakes. See yourself as I see you. Come, spend time with Me and let Me show you how much I treasure you and love you.

Do not be afraid; you will not be put to shame. Do not fear disgrace;
you will not be humiliated. You will forget the shame of your youth and
remember no more the reproach of your widowhood.

—Isaiah 54:4

SEPTEMBER 26

I created you solely to be My child. You are not an orphan. I am your Father and your home is with Me. You will never be alone, for you belong to Me. You do not have to act right, dress right, talk right, or do right in order for Me to accept and love you. I want you to feel valued, honored, accepted and loved solely because I created you. You don't have to prove yourself. Embrace this reality and these truths. Come, enjoy being My child and rest in My loving arms.

Yet to all who did receive him, to those who believed in his name,
he gave the right to become children of God.

—John 1:12

I will not leave you as orphans; I will come to you.

—John 14:18

SEPTEMBER 27

I am Almighty God. My power reigns within you because you know Me. It is a power unlike what you would possess on your own strength or merit. I want you to become aware of this power that is contained in you. Focus on it and call it forth. When you struggle with being kind or loving, access My love within you. When you're hung up with resentment, draw from My source already in you to let it go. When you are angry, allow My peace to overtake you and fill you up. Please know that My power is there for you in every situation you face. In all times, quiet yourself before Me and allow Me to share My heart with you. I continually walk with you through hardships and times in the wilderness with My loving arms sustaining you and giving you comfort. I love you that much. Become aware of Me guiding you, speaking to you softly in your thoughts, revealing the lies and negative thoughts and giving you clear vision concerning My ways. Welcome Me into your life and allow My presence to work in you and flow through you. Your goal does not have to be just to get through life, but let your goal be to live life filled with My peace, contentment, and joy!

We continually ask God to fill you with the knowledge of his will through all the wisdom and understanding that the Spirit gives, so that you may live a life worthy of the Lord and please him in every way: bearing fruit in every good work, growing in the knowledge of God, being strengthened with all power according to his glorious might so that you may have great endurance and patience.

—Colossians 1:9b-11

SEPTEMBER 28

*N*ever get comfortable in your walk with Me, thinking that you are invincible from the snare of the enemy or that you can't be lured away because you are following My ways. That thinking is rooted in pride. Even though I have overcome the enemy, his ways are subtle and crafty. Be on guard at all times protecting your heart and mind. Stay alert and clear minded. Bathe everything in prayer and stay connected to Me constantly. I have overcome the enemy and nothing can change that.

Be on guard! Be alert! You do not know when that time will come.

—Mark 13:33

Above all else, guard your heart, for everything you do flows from it.

—Proverbs 4:23

*Y*ou are busy doing things for Me, but do you really know Me? Are you focused on memorizing Scriptures, making sure you get your prayers in, or lending a hand to others? They are all wonderful things for you to continue to do, but please don't let these things take the place of putting your relationship with Me as your first priority. I want you to spend time in My presence, recalling what you know about My nature that you read in My Word and write it on your heart. Share with Me what you would share with a trusted friend. Enjoy the peace in being still before Me and feeling My presence. This is pleasing to Me and of great worth.

*And without faith it is impossible to please God, because anyone who comes
to him must believe that he exists and that he rewards those who earnestly seek him.*
—Hebrews 11:6

*Jesus answered, "I am the way and the truth and the life.
No one comes to the Father except through me."*
—John 14:6

*S*ometimes you feel like you're in the minority following Me. You watch friends go about their lives without a thought of Me, and they seem happy and prosperous to you, not seeming to have any issues or struggles. You wonder if it is really worth the work it takes to mature spiritually and to take the time to pray and read your Bible. It's tempting to just do what you want to do without regard to Me. My child, don't fall for the subtle deception of the enemy. Those are all lies you are believing. People can wear a mask to hide what is really going on inside. People may also seem to be getting away with not having Me in their lives, but there is a big price to pay at the end. Please don't fall into the trap of the enemy. Persevere and don't be deceived! You know the ending.

*Follow my example, as I follow the example of Christ. I praise you for remembering
me in everything and for holding to the traditions just as I passed them on to you.*
—1 Corinthians 11:1-2

*For God so loved the world that he gave his one and only Son,
that whoever believes in him shall not perish but have eternal life.*
—John 3:16

OCTOBER 1

*Y*ou think you don't struggle with pride or that you have overcome it. Pride is one of the biggest obstacles in a relationship with Me. When you try to do things on your own or when you won't let anyone share in your struggles, that shows pride. When you are too busy to show kindness, or if you are a perfectionist, or if you avoid people you don't want to associate with, that shows pride. Pride comes from inside the heart. A proud person thinks of themselves as higher than another. It takes the glory that is intended for Me and keeps it for yourself. Pride says that you can do it better than someone else. Pride gives yourself the credit for something that I have done. It is so easily woven into a person's life and must be kept in check. When you realize you have been prideful, repent, turn away from it and look to Me. Ask Me to show you when you are prideful and I will help you. Beware of pride, for it can infect many of the decisions you make. I detest pride.

To fear the Lord is to hate evil; I hate pride and arrogance, evil behavior and perverse speech.
—Proverbs 8:13

In his pride the wicked man does not seek him, in all his thoughts there is no room for God.
—Psalm 10:4

OCTOBER 2

*B*ecause of the cross, Satan is a defeated foe, and sin has no control over you. You have the power to resist temptation and to not go back to your old ways of living life apart from Me. Your thought life does not have any control over you either as you choose to let go of the lies. Your strength and source of power come from Me. You cannot fail when your eyes are on Me. You are not an orphan but My dearly loved and cherished child. That knowledge alone is empowering. Your destiny is firmly rooted in My perfect love and truth and no situation or trial can sway you. Write these truths on your heart.

His divine power has granted to us all things that pertain to life and godliness, through the knowledge of him who called us to his own glory and excellence, by which he has granted to us his precious and very great promises, so that through them you may become partakers of the divine nature, having escaped from the corruption that is in the world because of sinful desire.
—2 Peter 1:3-4 (ESV)

OCTOBER 3

You have been living your life in a way that you know is not pleasing to Me, yet you feel you can't help it. As a result, you are pulling away from Me, wondering how I could love you or want to help. The guilt and shame you feel because of this thinking weigh you down. My child, those are lies you are believing. It is the subtle lie of the enemy who wants to destroy you. Please don't pull away from Me, especially when making these wrong choices. Instead, come closer and allow Me to give you what you need to make the changes you know you need to make. I see your actions, but I would never leave you. Instead, it brings tears to My eyes because I know the pain you are in by making these choices. Let Me walk with you, giving you support and help to guide your way.

So I find this law at work: Although I want to do good, evil is right there with me. For in my inner being I delight in God's law; but I see another law at work in me, waging war against the law of my mind and making me a prisoner of the law of sin at work within me. What a wretched man I am! Who will rescue me from this body that is subject to death? Thanks be to God, who delivers me through Jesus Christ our Lord!
—Romans 7:21-25

OCTOBER 4

My nature is that I am good and that I am light, love, hope, peace, joy and life. This is the essence of who I am, and I can't be anything that opposes this. I freely and lovingly give these gifts to you if you choose to receive them. As you go deeper into a relationship with Me and remain there, the more you will get to know Me and be able to trust Me enough to give total control of your life to Me. When you are in My loving arms, you can give Me all of your burdens and leave them there. Then you can rest in My presence and focus only on Me as I work out all the challenges in your life. How freeing that is! This is who I am to you. Won't you embrace it?

This is the message we have heard from him and declare to you: God is light; in him there is no darkness at all.
—1 John 1:5

Every good and perfect gift is from above, coming down from the Father of the heavenly lights, who does not change like shifting shadows.
—James 1:17

$\mathcal{M}$y heart for you is to be awakened to the wonder of being in My presence. I want you to know that I am here with you and that this knowledge changes your life. Imagine seeing My Son, Jesus, in His glory and splendor, standing in the room with you. Imagine Him in front of you looking into your eyes, lovingly taking hold of your hands and saying, "It will be all right. I am here for you and will give you what you need. For I give you hope". Imagine His love pouring into you and feeling His peace and strength flowing into you as well. Pause and take it in … and see how it changes your outlook. As you draw closer, keeping your focus on Jesus, you suddenly realize that nothing you are facing matters, except gazing at Him and staying in His glory! Imagine His joy that He also pours into you— a joy you have never experienced before, joy in spite of all of your griefs. How amazing it is to experience His love and joy like that. My child, this isn't something you just imagine. This is My reality for you, My "right now" reality! Jesus is here with you, giving you all these things. This is My heart for you— to experience and know My love for you. My heart for you is to experience My love and presence all the time. I desire you to be lost in the wonder of My love and presence.

One thing I ask from the Lord, this only do I seek: that I may dwell in the house of the Lord all the days of my life, to gaze on the beauty of the Lord and to seek him in his temple.
—Psalm 27:4

$\mathcal{W}$hen you place your trust in Me, you develop confidence in Me. The confidence is an expectation that who I am to you and what My Word says is real and can be trusted. Rest in this knowledge. This confidence is a good thing and very pleasing to Me. Please guard your heart from becoming confident in yourself and your own abilities apart from Me. Pride can come on as a subtle deception. Stay connected so you don't lose that confidence in Me by becoming influenced by sin. Have no confidence in anything apart from Me. Live out your life trusting in Me, because it is then you put the power in My hands and I won't fail you. That is My promise to you.

Being confident of this, that he who began a good work in you will carry it on to completion until the day of Christ Jesus.
—Philippians 1:6

For the Lord will be your confidence and will keep your foot from being caught.
—Proverbs 3:26 (ESV)

OCTOBER 7

*P*ursue joy at all costs. Make it a life goal. Look for joy in each day and in every situation that arises. It is a command that you find in My Word. The purpose of choosing joy is to transform your life and to glorify Me. When you pursue joy, you have a positive focus and you leave behind the challenges as you turn your eyes upward to Me and connect to what I am doing in your life. Joy only comes from Me and is My gift to you. Become a living expression of My joy and pass it on to others.

Further, my brothers and sisters, rejoice in the Lord! It is no trouble for me
to write the same things to you again, and it is a safeguard for you.
—Philippians 3:1

But may the righteous be glad and rejoice before God; may they be happy and joyful.
—Psalm 68:3

OCTOBER 8

*T*here are many things you have the freedom to do and experience. But be aware that not everything is beneficial for you. Too much of any good thing, including eating, drinking or shopping, for instance, can be excessive and harmful. Things that are harmless for most people, if not guarded, could become a temptation or get out of control. Be aware if your actions would harm a fellow believer or yourself. Be cautious of the subtle deception when something you do that is harmless in moderation becomes an addiction. Guard against finding yourself in a position that would compromise your relationship with someone of the opposite sex. Always be on guard; the enemy looks for a weak spot. But remember, I am here to give you strength when you are tempted to cross the line. You are never alone.

"I have the right to do anything," you say—but not everything is beneficial.
"I have the right to do anything"—but I will not be mastered by anything.
—1 Corinthians 6:12

Do not love the world or anything in the world. If anyone loves the world,
love for the Father is not in them. For everything in the world—the lust of the flesh,
the lust of the eyes, and the pride of life—comes not from the Father but from the world.
The world and its desires pass away, but whoever does the will of God lives forever.
—1 John 2:15-17

*Y*ou are living in the supernatural kingdom. Your salvation is supernatural. Your birth is supernatural. Did you ever think of it that way? You are empowered to do what My Son did. It isn't just for the very religious or just for pastors; it is for all those who know Me as their Savior and Lord. I empower you with My authority to pray for the sick and heal them in My name, to bring deliverance and inner healing, to bind up the brokenhearted and to proclaim the Good News to all who will hear. Do all these things in My name to bring Me glory. Be My obedient vessel and witness to accomplish the work for My Kingdom. This is who I made you to be!

The Spirit of the Lord is on me, because he has anointed me to proclaim good news to the poor. He has sent me to proclaim freedom for the prisoners and recovery of sight for the blind, to set the oppressed free.

—Luke 4:18

*Y*our aim as you pursue maturity in Me is to be in My will. The most important thing you can do is to have a personal relationship with Me. I also created you in My image for a specific purpose. Seek out this purpose. I have given you gifts and abilities to use in service to Me. I want you to be My disciple and be committed to following Me daily, whatever the cost, knowing all the while I empower and equip you and want the best for you. You learn about My will through My Word and by being guided by the Holy Spirit. Learn to trust Me and step out in faith with My Word giving you the security and confidence you need. The safest and most secure place to be is in the center of My will, for it gives you total peace.

Do not conform to the pattern of this world, but be transformed by the renewing of your mind. Then you will be able to test and approve what God's will is—his good, pleasing and perfect will.
—Romans 12:2

There are different kinds of gifts, but the same Spirit distributes them. There are different kinds of service, but the same Lord. There are different kinds of working, but in all of them and in everyone it is the same God at work.

—1 Corinthians 12:4-6

OCTOBER 11

*I*n a split second your life is changed. There may not be any warning. At first you are in a state of shock, and then negative thoughts start flooding your mind. You feel sick to your stomach and totally out of control as though you are in a bad nightmare. Fear grips your mind. I know it is hard but, now more than ever, keep focusing on Me instead of what you are going through. When you don't know how to pray, just cry out to Me. You may feel as if I am not listening, but please don't go by your feelings. I am right here with you; My Word guarantees this. Please understand that My ways are not your ways, nor is My timing your timing. But I am all you need, for I am enough! I may not answer your prayers the way you want Me to, but I see the total picture and answer in a way that is My best for you. Ask Me to guard your mind, health and heart. I am here to relieve the pain of sorrow, brokenness and despair and to offer you My peace that you can experience regardless of what you are dealing with!

I remain confident of this: I will see the goodness of the Lord in the land of the living. Wait for the Lord; be strong and take heart and wait for the Lord.
—Psalm 27:13-14

OCTOBER 12

*C*ome, worship Me and spend time in My presence. I want to open your heart to receive Me. Let go of anything getting in the way of all I have for you. Take time and feel My love and goodness being poured into you…. It is so pleasing to Me when you take the time to seek Me more deeply. I want you to feel Me hold you in My strong, protective arms, as you realize I am with you, guiding and providing for you. Feel the peace I am giving you as you learn to rest in Me instead of trying to be in control of everything. Being in My presence is a great place to rest and linger. May your heart burn for more of Me, for that is My heart's desire for you.

I have given them the glory that you gave me, that they may be one as we are one—I in them and you in me—so that they may be brought to complete unity. Then the world will know that you sent me and have loved them even as you have loved me.
—John 17:22-23

Humble yourselves, therefore, under God's mighty hand, that he may lift you up in due time. Cast all your anxiety on him because he cares for you.
—1 Peter 5:6-7

OCTOBER 13

*I*t is My nature to be good. Everything about Me is full of goodness. I formed and created you and so I know you intimately. I know just what you need even better than you do. As you pursue Me and as I call you deeper, you will come to know Me as your Daddy, your perfect Daddy—your loving, trustworthy, dependable, ever present Daddy. I am a Daddy who never will let you down, who is your greatest cheerleader and who wants only the best for you. You are a dearly loved child, loved by your Heavenly Daddy. Embrace your identity.

The Spirit you received does not make you slaves, so that you live in fear again; rather, the Spirit you received brought about your adoption to sonship. And by him we cry, "Abba, Father." The Spirit himself testifies with our spirit that we are God's children.
—Romans 8:15-16

See what great love the Father has lavished on us, that we should be called children of God! And that is what we are! The reason the world does not know us is that it did not know him.
—1 John 3:1

OCTOBER 14

The most important thing for you to do in your life is to love Me with all of your heart, soul, mind and strength. You sometimes wonder how you really accomplish that. I want you to love, adore and serve Me with everything that you are, including your emotions, spirit, actions, thoughts and your inmost commitments. That means keeping Me in the forefront of your thoughts where nothing is larger in your mind than the awareness of My presence. It is through the witness of My faithfulness during times of struggle and trial that a deep love for Me begins to blossom. By getting to know My nature better, your love for Me will grow. When you truly love Me, you will honor and revere Me, and you will pay close attention to and obey My desires found in My Word. I will be on your mind constantly and nothing else in life will matter more than your relationship with Me. It's a great place to be!

"Of all the commandments, which is the most important?" "The most important one," answered Jesus, "is this: Love the Lord your God with all your heart and with all your soul and with all your mind and with all your strength."
—Mark 12:28a-30

*N*ext to loving Me, the second most important thing for you to do is to love your neighbor as yourself. Love others to reflect how you love yourself. Make sure you have in place a godly love for yourself. If you have trouble loving yourself, look at the identity Scriptures which illustrate how I love you and how I see you. Think to yourself how you would like to be honored, respected and treated; and work out of that mindset. Be cautious about being tempted to treat others as you have been treated especially if it was in opposition of how I treat you. There is no place for rudeness, revenge, or misuse of power. You sometimes wonder how to accomplish loving others as yourself. To love others, look for positive ways to enhance their lives and prosperity. Pray a blessing on them and be honest, merciful, just, kind and gracious. Make it a central focus of your life to reach out to your neighbors. Your neighbor is everyone you come in contact with. How you treat others is a statement of your Christian character and your witness to others as well as your gift to Me.

The second is this: 'Love your neighbor as yourself.' There is no commandment greater than these.
—Mark 12:31

*Y*ou suddenly find yourself in a situation that you have no control over, didn't want to be in and have no idea what to do. Fear takes over and is paralyzing. You are overwhelmed and feel defeated and hopeless. My child, turn to Me and allow Me to help. Stop thinking about what has happened and take those thoughts captive. Don't look back at what was or could have been or should be. Don't look to the side at the "what if's" or all the obstacles or impossibilities. Look straight at Me, walk on water with Me and do not waiver. Keep your eyes focused on Me and who I am to you! This is where all your Bible reading and spending time with Me helps tremendously because you really have gotten to know Me and are able to put your trust in Me for such a time as this. If you haven't been doing these things, start now. It really helps to have a personal relationship with Me to quicken your faith and trust. I will give you one step at a time to take and will walk with you, hand in hand.

Finally, brothers and sisters, whatever is true, whatever is noble, whatever is right, whatever is pure, whatever is lovely, whatever is admirable—if anything is excellent or praiseworthy—think about such things. —Philippians 4:8

OCTOBER 17

*H*ave you ever felt lonely even though you have family and friends? Loneliness can be crippling both spiritually and emotionally. I have created you for companionship both with Me and with others. I encourage you to admit that you feel lonely. Don't try to deny it or run from it. There is nothing wrong with having this normal human feeling. Even My Son felt alone! But please don't dwell on it, for then you fall into Satan's snare. Purposefully pursue godly friendships with people who will laugh, cry, encourage you and are there to pray with you and point you to Me. Join a group at your church or volunteer at a place where you can help and encourage others less fortunate. I encourage you to pursue a deeper relationship with Me, also. Feeling My love for you will force the loneliness out of your life. Don't run away from Me by pursuing temporary fixes. Run towards Me!

One who has unreliable friends soon comes to ruin,
but there is a friend who sticks closer than a brother.

—Proverbs 18:24

My eyes are ever on the Lord, for only he will release my feet from the snare.
Turn to me and be gracious to me, for I am lonely and afflicted. Relieve
the troubles of my heart and free me from my anguish.

—Psalm 25:15-17

OCTOBER 18

I want you to honor your loved ones and those around you. Show them respect and guard their dignity. Learn to see their hearts the way I see their hearts. See them as My children whom I created with perfection and love with all of My heart. When they mess up, please don't judge. Just acknowledge to yourself that this is what they look like when they mess up. Let there be no condemnation on your part, just as there is no condemnation from Me when you mess up. Give them grace and show mercy. It's not always easy to do this but persevere and know that it is a process. It is My heart's desire for you to honor others.

Honor all people, love the brotherhood, fear God, honor the king.

—1 Peter 2:17 (NASB)

Be devoted to one another in love. Honor one another above yourselves.

—Romans 12:10

OCTOBER 19

*T*hroughout your busy day, remember to take time to quiet your mind and connect your spirit to My spirit. When you are in conflict, pause, be still and connect to My loving presence. This may be new to you, but it is worth the work. There may be times you don't feel anything and wonder if it is worth the effort, but it is. Even though you may not feel or experience anything, something is happening in the heavenly realm and in your inner being. In time you will notice a difference. It is then that you will have clarity of mind and purpose. You will discern My heart and My will for you. You will find peace and contentment. You will find strength and be encouraged. Please, stay connected to Me.

Remain in me, as I also remain in you. No branch can bear fruit by itself; it must remain in the vine. Neither can you bear fruit unless you remain in me. "I am the vine; you are the branches. If you remain in me and I in you, you will bear much fruit; apart from me you can do nothing."
—John 15:4-5

OCTOBER 20

*M*y heart for you is not to just know of Me, like you know of the president or of a famous movie star. I want you to really know Me, the essence of Me. I want you to know who I am, My character and nature which you will find in My Word and by spending time in My presence. My heart for you is not to remain there but to go even deeper. I want you to walk with Me daily in all that you do. This means you seek My will for you in everything as you ask Me for My thoughts, opinions, direction and for you to stay in continuous communication with Me. It becomes a way of life, where nothing is more important than My will for you and your relationship with Me. I want you to trust Me enough to walk on water with Me, not focusing on anything other than My best for you. It is an act of utter dependence, submission and trust! Paul said it best where he counted everything else as worthless in comparison to that tremendous blessing of knowing Me intimately. Will you come to that place, too, and follow My heart for you? Watch what will happen as you surrender your life to My will for you!

But whatever gain I had, I counted as loss for the sake of Christ. Indeed, I count everything as loss because of the surpassing worth of knowing Christ Jesus my Lord. For his sake I have suffered the loss of all things and count them as rubbish, in order that I may gain Christ and be found in him, not having a righteousness of my own that comes from the law, but that which comes through faith in Christ, the righteousness from God that depends on faith.
—Philippians 3:7-9 (ESV)

OCTOBER 21

$\mathcal{T}$oday is the day I have created just for you. It is full of My blessings and promises to you. All around you, My goodness is displayed. Purposely look with your spiritual eyes for this wonder. I want you to find joy in this day that is especially made for you and choose to be glad in it all day long. This conscious choice keeps your focus on Me, My goodness and what I am doing in your life whether you can see it or not. It changes the way you think and look at things. It lines things up with My ways and will make a huge difference as you learn to reprogram your thinking. Find the joy and goodness in each and every day. No matter what the circumstances, there is always something to be thankful for. You will be blessed with this new way of thinking.

This is the day which the Lord has made; let us rejoice and be glad in it.
—Psalm 118:24 (NASB)

There, in the presence of the Lord your God, you and your families shall eat and shall rejoice in everything you have put your hand to, because the Lord your God has blessed you.
—Deuteronomy 12:7

OCTOBER 22

$\mathcal{S}$eek after My heart and be relentless about it. Please know this is of great importance to Me. My ways are so different from what you are used to observing. Your first reaction to a situation or person should not be judgment or condemnation. Eliminate this from your life. Instead, open your eyes to see their brokenness, hurt and pain. Show compassion and grace regardless of what you are receiving from them. Bathe them in love, for My love speaks volumes. Love penetrates hearts in ways that nothing else can. Watch what love can do!

But love your enemies, do good to them, and lend to them without expecting to get anything back. Then your reward will be great, and you will be children of the Most High, because he is kind to the ungrateful and wicked. Be merciful, just as your Father is merciful.
—Luke 6:35-36

OCTOBER 23

$\mathcal{L}$oneliness may be a part of your life right now, or it could be in the future. No one is exempt from it. It can happen suddenly or sneak up on you. There is a difference between being alone and being lonely. Being alone means you are by yourself with no one there with you. In contrast, loneliness is a state of mind, where you can feel you have no one to talk to, no one to turn to, or no one who really cares. This can happen even if you are married or surrounded by family. If it happens to you, turn to Me right away. Turn to Me and away from your feelings. I understand your feelings and can give you comfort. Let go of the lies you believe that it will always be this way, that you can't go on like this and that no one cares. These thoughts are not from Me but from the enemy who wants to destroy you. Turn your attention outward and help someone in need. Open yourself up to new connections and new groups. Let Me strengthen you, build your character and give you a whole new outlook. Remember, My Son went through loneliness, too. He did it for you and for your victory over this!

He was despised and rejected by mankind, a man of suffering, and familiar with pain.
Like one from whom people hide their faces he was despised, and we held him in low esteem.
—Isaiah 53:3

OCTOBER 24

$\mathcal{M}$y gifts to you are eternal life with Me forever and a life full of peace, joy and contentment here on earth if you choose it. There is nothing you can do to deserve this gift. You were worth My Son dying. I find great value in you no matter what your age is or what your history was. I see the hidden treasure in you and call forth your potential. Your future is bright with My wonderful promises to claim as your own. With your eyes on Me, all fear vanishes as you walk in confidence with Me by your side, guiding your path. Be bold in Me and walk into your destiny.

The thief comes only to steal and kill and destroy;
I have come that they may have life, and have it to the full.
—John 10:10

Every good and perfect gift is from above, coming down from the
Father of the heavenly lights, who does not change like shifting shadows.
—James 1:17

*B*ecome awakened to a love relationship with Me and with your Bible. I want to create a desire and a hunger in you for wanting to read My Word. May it become more important to you than your desire for food so that it may nourish you and feed your soul. May My Word breathe life into your body. I know you really do want this, but if you're honest, the desire is as far as it goes and you often fail to carry through. There is no condemnation from Me, but I want you to know it does grieve Me because I watch you deal with pain that you wouldn't need to deal with. I know how much your life would be enhanced if you would feed on My Word daily. Open your heart to what is important to Me, and unite it with Mine.

Keep this Book of the Law always on your lips; meditate on it day and night, so that you may be careful to do everything written in it. Then you will be prosperous and successful.
—Joshua 1:8

Jesus answered, "It is written: Man shall not live on bread alone, but on every word that comes from the mouth of God."
—Matthew 4:4

*T*ake time to worship Me. Give Me your honor, glory and praise. In these precious and intimate times, I don't want you to ask for anything but simply worship Me in spirit and in truth. I invite you to come up to the throne room where you will see My presence with your spiritual eyes, surrounded by indescribable sights and angelic sounds. You will be awe-struck as you stand in wonder at My Holy Presence! I want to awaken you to how your praises to Me will move both My heart and your heart as you worship Me spirit to spirit, heart to heart. I pause to listen to every one of your prayers and praises and they move Me to tears. My heart pours out on you pure love and gratitude. Receive it.

Yet a time is coming and has now come when the true worshipers will worship the Father in the Spirit and in truth, for they are the kind of worshipers the Father seeks. God is spirit, and his worshipers must worship in the Spirit and in truth.
—John 4:23-24

Through Jesus, therefore, let us continually offer to God a sacrifice of praise—the fruit of lips that openly profess his name.
—Hebrews 13:15

*T*here is a place deep within you that is guarded. It is a place where fear, pride, brokenness and lies reign. You may not even be aware of this place. You don't let anyone in there. This grieves Me when you won't let Me in. It breaks My heart. It may be that you don't want to bother Me, thinking others have bigger problems, or that you are choosing to stay in control out of fear, or that the strongholds are holding you tight. Oh, My child, open your heart to Me. Trust in Me, My precious one. Allow Me to touch your heart and soul, to share with you My truth and pour out My power. My loving touch brings healing, restoration and refreshment. It lifts the heavy burdens that you no longer have to carry and will give you a peace that you have not felt before. Please allow Me in to help you.

He answered, "I heard you in the garden, and I was afraid because I was naked; so I hid."
—Genesis 3:10

Peace I leave with you; my peace I give you. I do not give to you as the world gives.
Do not let your hearts be troubled and do not be afraid.
—John 14:27

*D*o you have confidence in Me? Do you really believe the Bible to be true? If you intentionally follow My Word, do you have confidence in the outcome? When the big problems rear their ugly heads, are you resting in My truth? I know you still struggle with this and then feel guilty. It's all right to have those doubts, but if you dwell on them and get stuck in unbelief, that is not all right. When you recognize the thought, renounce it as a lie. Take any thought captive that would hinder your confidence in Me. Guard your heart at all cost. Focus on increasing your confidence in Me and rest in My ability to be Lord of your life.

My message and my preaching were not with wise and persuasive words,
but with a demonstration of the Spirit's power, so that your faith might
not rest on human wisdom, but on God's power.
—1 Corinthians 2:4-5

For it is we who are the circumcision, we who serve God by his Spirit,
who boast in Christ Jesus, and who put no confidence in the flesh.
—Philippians 3:3

*M*y child, I yearn for you to come deeper, deeper into a relationship with Me. I want you to realize it is My very breath in your lungs and My power in your body. It is My encouragement to your wavering heart, My restoration to your weary soul and My healing to your aging body. I give you life that man can not give you. I am your source of strength and guidance. No matter what situation you face, I am there watching over you and encouraging you. I walk you through the worries and fears that you face. I give you abundant life. I want to restore you, give you hope and mend your troubled heart. Come, walk with Me daily and put your trust in Me.

What agreement is there between the temple of God and idols?
For we are the temple of the living God. As God has said: "I will live with them
and walk among them, and I will be their God, and they will be my people."
—2 Corinthians 6:16

Come near to God and he will come near to you. Wash your hands,
you sinners, and purify your hearts, you double-minded.
—James 4:8

*M*y presence is all around you and My glory fills the room you are in. I want you to become aware of this reality. I am not some distant, impersonal God who just says and does things at random or on a whim. I am never too busy to be there for you and no problem you deal with is too insignificant or small for Me to be concerned about. I care about every detail of your life and anxiously wait for you to come to Me. I want you to realize how much I love you and that I really do yearn for you to turn to Me with everything you face. I can make your journey easier and lighter and can take away your heavy load. You may still walk through a difficult situation, but with Me by your side, it changes your perspective. Let Me fill you with My power, peace and strength. Feel My presence as I walk with you every day. You will be amazed at the transformation as you find My peace in the midst of a storm.

The Lord replied, "My Presence will go with you, and I will give you rest."
—Exodus 33:14

You will seek me and find me when you seek me with all your heart.
—Jeremiah 29:13

OCTOBER 31

*Y*ou find yourself in a situation that you didn't ask for or want to be in. The timing for any closure of this is unknown. You go about each day putting out fires or trying to keep your head above water. Each day there seem to be new challenges or obstacles. You are trying to stay focused on Me, but you are tired physically and emotionally, and part of you just wants to give up. I know this is a difficult time, but it is at this precise time you need to stay connected with Me the most! Your mind wants to succumb to the lies and enticement of the enemy, who is working overtime to ensnare you. Don't give in but stand firm. It will be hard work, but continually give Me your focus. Refocus every time you become aware that your thoughts are not from Me. I am here to hold you up and to give you encouragement. I am the Lord of every obstacle. Recall how in the past everything worked out, maybe not exactly as you wanted it to but it always worked out. Recall how I've answered your prayers. Think about what I am doing that you can't see. Connect to My strength that I am pouring into you to sustain you physically and emotionally. I am right there with you, supporting you and never leaving your side. We will see this through together. Hold on to the hope I give you!

And the God of all grace, who called you to his eternal glory in Christ, after you have suffered a little while, will himself restore you and make you strong, firm and steadfast.
—1 Peter 5:10

Blessed is the one who perseveres under trial because, having stood the test, that person will receive the crown of life that the Lord has promised to those who love him.
—James 1:12

*W*hat do you do with My promises you read about in the Bible? Do you dismiss them because you believe it is true for others but couldn't be true for you? Do you think, "Wow, that's a really great promise and is encouraging," but then as time goes by, you forget all about it? My child, these promises are there because they are very real and are in place so you can experience abundant life in Me. Please don't entertain thoughts that are contrary to My truths. It is important that you understand what I think of you in order for you to bring your destiny into reality. Please don't think about yourself differently from how I see you. You were born to touch others with My love and to experience life abundantly.

I will not forget you! See, I have engraved you on the palms of my hands; your walls are ever before me.
—Isaiah 49:15b-16a

And my God will meet all your needs according to the riches of his glory in Christ Jesus.
—Philippians 4:19

*C*ome to Me in boldness of faith, with a humble and surrendered heart. You have gotten to know Me through My Word and spending time with Me. You have slowly allowed Me into your secret place, that until now has been kept from Me because of pride, fear, or doubt. You realize nothing is hidden from Me, and you don't have to feel bad because I know your heart. You want to surrender your life and let Me be Lord of it, but you want this to be meaningful and real to you so you're taking steps in the right direction to be fully committed to your decision to surrender everything. I honor that, and it gives Me joy. It is a process, though. I ask you gently, "What is holding you back? What have you not let go of yet? Where is the conflict?" Know who I am and how much I love you. Take the step of faith and give Me your all.

Then Jesus said to his disciples, "Whoever wants to be my disciple must deny themselves and take up their cross and follow me. For whoever wants to save their life will lose it, but whoever loses their life for me will find it."
—Matthew 16:24-25

*C*ome and learn to live your life from glory to glory as you focus on Me and have your dwelling place in Me. It is then My glory surrounds you and permeates you. You are connected to My power and presence and operate in the fruit of the spirit. It's all part of going from glory to glory. You feel My peace; you hear Me communicate with you. You know without a doubt I am sovereign and want the best for you. As you continue to live from glory to glory, you are always connected, always confident in who I am to you. You still may disconnect from Me unknowingly or by choice, and then you live from worry to worry. But it isn't long before you reconnect. It is where you have chosen to be once you experience living from My glory to glory. You won't want anything else. You realize the splendor of this gift, and it's worth surrendering to!

And we all, who with unveiled faces contemplate the Lord's glory, are being transformed into his image with ever-increasing glory, which comes from the Lord, who is the Spirit.
—2 Corinthians 3:18

His divine power has given us everything we need for a godly life through our knowledge of him who called us by his own glory and goodness.
—2 Peter 1:3

NOVEMBER 4

*C*ome spend time with Me. Drink from My living waters. Drink in My love, My glory and My life and be filled to overflowing. Tarry here for a while, being totally immersed in My splendor. Come away refreshed, renewed, empowered. Take what I give you, and pass it on to others. Be My light to a dark world, My encouragement to the weary and My love to those who don't know Me. Repeat this cycle. Be filled and then pour out. That warms My heart.

"Let anyone who is thirsty come to me and drink. Whoever believes in me, as Scripture has said, rivers of living water will flow from within them."
—John 7:37b-38

Heal the sick, raise the dead, cleanse those who have leprosy, drive out demons. Freely you have received; freely give.
—Matthew 10:8b

$\mathcal{D}$o you experience fear? What are you afraid of? Does it keep you from being able to do something or hold you back? It can be paralyzing, keeping you stuck in a situation thinking there is no way out. Please know that fear is not from Me. When you believe something is going to go wrong or believe the "what if's", you are putting your faith in the enemy whose goal is to steal, kill and destroy. My child, I don't condemn you. I reveal this to you out of My love for you. It grieves Me when you live out of fear. Satan wants to keep you from receiving My blessings. Choose the better way. When you realize you are walking in fear, stop, take that thought captive and put your focus on Me. Recall My promises to you, who I am to you, what I've done for you in the past and choose to place your faith in Me. Jesus conquered your fear at the cross. Live from peace as you trust in Me.

When I am afraid, I put my trust in you.

—Psalm 56:3

For God gave us a spirit not of fear but of power and love and self-control.
—2 Timothy 1:7 (ESV)

$\mathcal{A}$waken each day with a song on your heart. May I be the first thing on your mind. I give you this day as a gift so rejoice in it. Look for My goodness all around you, for it is there. Keep looking until you find it. Look for My sovereignty in every situation you face. I am there with you. Don't linger on negative thoughts or feelings. Give them all to Me and think about what I am doing in you instead. Rest in My arms, giving Me all of your burdens. Rest, with My peace flowing through you.

This is the day that the Lord has made; let us rejoice and be glad in it.
—Psalm 118:24 (ESV)

Rejoice in the Lord always. I will say it again: Rejoice!
—Philippians 4:4

$\mathcal{W}$hen you feel discouraged, stressed, or fearful, admit to yourself that you are weak and not perfect. In the world's eyes that might be a negative thing to admit, but in My eyes it shows strength and character. It is only after this revelation that you are free to let go of control and turn to Me. Celebrate your weakness because then My power may rest in you. I have all the strength and power you need. My power is made perfect in your weakness. Be encouraged.

But he said to me, "My grace is sufficient for you, for my power is made perfect in weakness." Therefore I will boast all the more gladly about my weaknesses, so that Christ's power may rest on me. That is why, for Christ's sake, I delight in weaknesses, in insults, in hardships, in persecutions, in difficulties. For when I am weak, then I am strong.
—2 Corinthians 12:9-10

NOVEMBER 8

$\mathcal{S}$eek contentment, for it is of great value. You won't find contentment in how the world seeks it, through having few problems or being successful. It isn't in having financial security, good health, or a loving family either. These are all wonderful blessings and may make you feel content, but take any of them away and the contentment is gone, too. I want you to seek what Paul found. Even bound in chains in a cold, dark dungeon of a prison, he wrote of learning the secret of being content in any and every situation. It is not found in things. This contentment is found in living out of your position as My dearly loved child. Pursue your understanding of just how much I love you. Get to know Me and who I am to you through My Word. Learn what it means to be My child. I am a loving Daddy who cares about you physically, emotionally and spiritually. Contentment comes when you seek and choose it. I will help you find it if you let Me. It is one of My many gifts to you.

I know what it is to be in need, and I know what it is to have plenty. I have learned the secret of being content in any and every situation, whether well fed or hungry, whether living in plenty or in want.
—Philippians 4:12

The Spirit himself testifies with our spirit that we are God's children.
—Romans 8:16

I'm calling you to a deeper level in knowing Me as your Lord. When you came to know Me, an exchange happened and you no longer lived, but I live in you. What that means is, I'm calling you to die to self. Let go of control, pride and your way of doing things. Let go of offense, impatience, anger, fear, unforgiveness and anything that keeps you from Me. Cease from trying and enter My rest. In the world's view, this all seems so harsh and demanding. But the world doesn't know Me as you do. You study My Word and spend time with Me. You are beginning to comprehend how wide and deep My love is for you, My precious, precious child. Won't you take the next step, let go of self and connect to My spirit that already lives in you? My spirit is your source of victory over everything you struggle with. I pour out My love into you so that you, in turn, can love others. I give you joy, peace, kindness and all the other fruit of the Spirit if you allow Me to work in your heart. Place your faith and trust in Me. Come, walk deeper and allow My spirit and power to flow out of you. Peace will reign.

I have been crucified with Christ and I no longer live, but Christ lives in me. The life I now live in the body, I live by faith in the Son of God, who loved me and gave himself for me.
—Galatians 2:20

*W*hen you are still before Me, all of your attention is on Me. There is nothing getting in the way between you and Me— nothing at all. It is here you really tune into My sovereignty, power and glory. You become focused on this transformation in the way you think and it becomes real to you. Trust wells up as do belief, peace, serenity, contentment and, in time, even joy. This is a process that isn't forced or hurried but takes time and work. Cease striving, let go and relax. Don't "do", just "BE"! By letting go of everything you hold on to, any lies, control, idols, or anything getting in the way, you are free to experience Me in the stillness of your soul, mind and heart.

Be still before the Lord and wait patiently for him; do not fret when people succeed in their ways, when they carry out their wicked schemes.
—Psalm 37:7

Now then, stand still and see this great thing the Lord is about to do before your eyes!
—1 Samuel 12:16

*J*am Almighty God. I have power and might over everything. I am God above all things with no limitations. This is important for you to comprehend and understand. I raised Jesus from the dead. I give you this same power and it is already in you! The problem is, I watch as you try to do things on your own strength, and you get frustrated and discouraged. That makes Me sad to watch. My child, please let Me show you the better way. Pause in the situation you face and connect to Me. Acknowledge that I am might and power. Ask for My power to flow into the situation. When patience, love, or forgiveness is required, allow Me to flow through you. I will not fail you. It's yours for the asking as you connect to Me.

And if the Spirit of him who raised Jesus from the dead is living in you,
he who raised Christ from the dead will also give life to your mortal bodies
because of his Spirit who lives in you. Therefore, brothers and sisters, we have an
obligation—but it is not to the flesh, to live according to it. For if you live according
to the flesh, you will die; but if by the Spirit you put to death the misdeeds of the body,
you will live. For those who are led by the Spirit of God are the children of God.
—Romans 8:11-14

*A*re you frustrated by always trying to do good, striving but never achieving, lacking peace and contentment, or feeling guilty about all the ways you're failing Me? This cycle keeps repeating itself and you feel there doesn't seem to be a solution. My child, you are striving for unattainable goals. The laws from the Old Testament were never part of My original plan. They were added after the broken fellowship and sin in the Garden of Eden. Because of My Son's work on the cross, I have provided a better way. Please don't try to do things on your own strength or through your own reasoning anymore. Come to Me and live out of your relationship with Me—where you step aside and allow Me to work in and through you.

Therefore, there is now no condemnation for those who are in Christ Jesus, because
through Christ Jesus the law of the Spirit who gives life has set you free from the
law of sin and death. For what the law was powerless to do because it was weakened by
the flesh, God did by sending his own Son in the likeness of sinful flesh to be a sin offering.
And so he condemned sin in the flesh, in order that the righteous requirement of the law
might be fully met in us, who do not live according to the flesh but according to the Spirit.
—Romans 8:1-4

*Y*ou find yourself in a situation where you are choosing to do something that is not pleasing to Me, even though you have walked with Me. You know it is wrong and you know it will hurt your loved ones; yet, you deliberately continue down that path. The temptation is strong in you, and you feel that you can't help yourself and maybe even that you deserve this pleasure. You feel that you are too far into this and can't let go. You also feel distant from Me because you think I have turned My back on you. Those are lies you are believing. It is not too late. Choose right now to repent; confess this sin and turn your back on it. Deliberately separate yourself from the temptation and stay focused on Me. Draw your strength and self-control from Me. Declare that you have been set free from this sin and that it no longer has a hold on you. I love you regardless of what you did and rejoice that you are choosing to repent. Come back to Me and be set free! There is work involved, but I am right there by your side—supporting you, encouraging you and giving you everything you need.

No temptation has overtaken you except what is common to mankind.
And God is faithful; he will not let you be tempted beyond what you can bear. But
when you are tempted, he will also provide a way out so that you can endure it.
—1 Corinthians 10:13

*L*oving others can be difficult either because they are hard to love or because they might have done something that hurt you. You want to love them because you know that is My will and is pleasing to Me. But you are really struggling with loving them. My child, tune in to My loving presence and power already inside you. You can't love on your own merit, but I can love that person through you. Allow My love to flow through you into that person. Stay connected to My presence and watch Me work in your life as you love that person with My love. You will find it amazing as you step out of the way and allow My power to work through you!

Dear friends, let us love one another, for love comes from God. Everyone
who loves has been born of God and knows God. Whoever does not love does
not know God, because God is love. This is how God showed his love among us:
He sent his one and only Son into the world that we might live through him.
—1 John 4:7-9

NOVEMBER 15

You are My vessel that holds and contains My spirit. You have My presence in your bodily temple. Are you aware of this reality? Pause a moment and meditate on this. Because you know Me, you are filled with My power and ability. This knowledge is both life-giving and life-changing! You no longer have to strive or do anything on your own ability or strength. You no longer need to feel frustrated or discouraged. Be diligent about staying connected to Me. Intentionally move aside and allow My power to flow through whatever situation you face. Do you need to show kindness? Allow My abundant kindness to flow out of you. Do you need self-control? Allow My power to be the self-control you desire. My power supply is endless and addresses everything you need for whatever you face. It is a new way of thinking! Instead of trying to do things on your own strength, connect to My spirit already in place for this very reason. Write this on your heart. I am your source of power and strength already filled up in your inmost being. Draw from My source, not your own.

Don't you know that you yourselves are God's temple and that God's Spirit dwells in your midst?
—1 Corinthians 3:16

Do you not know that your bodies are temples of the Holy Spirit,
who is in you, whom you have received from God? You are not your own;
you were bought at a price. Therefore honor God with your bodies.
—1 Corinthians 6:19-20

NOVEMBER 16

What kind of foundation have you built your life on? Is it built on human reasoning or wisdom, on self, or on conditional love? If so, things may be fine for a season, but eventually when a storm hits, the foundation will be shaken and eventually will crumble. Instead, build your foundation on a genuine, deepening and constant relationship with Me that cannot be shaken. Your footing is solid as you stand on My love and My promises to you. Build your life's foundation on Me.

As for everyone who comes to me and hears my words and puts them into practice,
I will show you what they are like. They are like a man building a house, who dug down
deep and laid the foundation on rock. When a flood came, the torrent struck that house
but could not shake it, because it was well built. But the one who hears my words and does
not put them into practice is like a man who built a house on the ground without a foundation.
The moment the torrent struck that house, it collapsed and its destruction was complete.
—Luke 6:47-49

*D*o you struggle with forgiving yourself? My child, you are forgiven if you confess the sin and choose to turn away from it. It's covered by My Son's blood. When you find yourself doing something over and over again, confess it and then clothe yourself in righteousness. Don't believe the condemning lies that you aren't forgiven. You have the choice of seeing yourself as a filthy sinner or decked in a robe of righteousness as I see you. I have forgiven and redeemed you. It is finished. Don't beat yourself up over committing the same sin over and over again. Ask for My help. You are a new creation in Me. I have already provided everything you need. Stay connected and focused on Me and watch how your struggling will lessen as you draw strength and confidence from My abilities and power working in you!

If we confess our sins, he is faithful and just and will
forgive us our sins and purify us from all unrighteousness. —1 John 1:9

Therefore, if anyone is in Christ, the new creation has come: The old has gone, the new is here! All
this is from God, who reconciled us to himself through Christ and gave us the ministry of reconcilia-
tion: that God was reconciling the world to himself in Christ, not counting people's sins against them.
—2 Corinthians 5:17-19a

*H*ave you ever been discouraged and felt like an obstacle was insurmountable? Or have you felt overwhelmed with a sense of worthlessness? This is a lie from the enemy who wants you to continue to focus on this. My child, I want you to see a different perspective. Look to Me rather than focusing on the situation that caused you to be discouraged. I see you as part of a chosen race, a royal priesthood, a holy nation. You are My child and belong to Me. This is your identity. Meditate on this truth to bring you out of your gloom. By doing this, it draws your attention away from the lies and focuses on Me and My working through your circumstance. It gives you hope. Know your identity, step into it, and focus on Me!

But you are a chosen people, a royal priesthood, a holy nation, God's special possession, that
you may declare the praises of him who called you out of darkness into his wonderful light.
—1 Peter 2:9

"For I know the plans I have for you," declares the Lord, "plans to
prosper you and not to harm you, plans to give you hope and a future."
—Jeremiah 29:11

NOVEMBER 19

$\mathcal{I}$will provide all of your needs from My abundance. That is My promise to you. I know you believe Me, yet you question it. You think if that is My promise, then how can all these bad things happen to people, and why do you struggle? Remember, My ways are different from your ways, and My thoughts are at a different level than yours. Stop a moment, and think about what you really need and what is most important. My servant Paul understood this. Even through all of the hardships that he endured, being chained in a cold dark dungeon, he realized what was important and wrote about these things- love, peace, contentment, and joy. You can't buy any of these things; they come from Me alone and are free if you choose them. No matter what you face, I am right there with you, with My loving support. Choose to focus on Me and My provision for you. Choose to seek out My peace and joy, leaving everything else behind, and you will find them.

And my God will meet all your needs according to the riches of his glory in Christ Jesus.
—Philippians 4:19

Look at the birds of the air; they do not sow or reap or store away in barns, and yet your heavenly Father feeds them. Are you not much more valuable than they?
—Matthew 6:26

NOVEMBER 20

$\mathcal{I}$know you are down on yourself at times. You think about your past and also the mistakes you made. My child, please don't entertain those thoughts any longer. They do nothing but pull you down, which is what Satan is after. Retrain your thinking to focus on Me. I am a God who restores and redeems. I look past the rough exterior and see potential. I see past where you came from and know where you are headed. I look into your heart to see what will come out of it. I look at all the cracks and dysfunction and see the beauty instead. I know you've experienced pain, but that pain can't stay when you step into My victory that is yours. I want you to see what I'm seeing and step into it!

Restore to me the joy of your salvation and grant me a willing spirit, to sustain me.
—Psalm 51:12

You who have shown me many troubles and distresses will revive me again, and will bring me up again from the depths of the earth. May You increase my greatness and turn to comfort me.
—Psalm 71:20-21 (NASB)

NOVEMBER 21

$\mathcal{B}$elieve in Me. Believe in My promises and who I am to you. Put your faith, hope and trust in My power working within you and through you. Doubt, fear and unbelief are not from Me and are not My ways. Please don't put your faith in your own abilities or in lies you are believing. This only keeps you from enjoying My provisions. It is not enough to know these things in your head, but draw them into your heart by spending time with Me and staying connected. My promises are real and unchanging. I always want the best for you and I live and reign within you!

And without faith it is impossible to please God, because anyone who comes to him must believe that he exists and that he rewards those who earnestly seek him.
—Hebrews 11:6

For we live by faith, not by sight.
—2 Corinthians 5:7

NOVEMBER 22

$\mathcal{S}$ometimes you find yourself in the wilderness where there is fear, uncertainty and maybe even despair. It is a place where choices can be made and different paths taken. It may be a transitional period where you decide to continue relying on yourself or choose to trust and rely on Me. My child, it is in this wilderness I want you to look to Me and realize I am beckoning you and waiting with loving arms wide open to receive you. Don't trust in your own strength to do things, but rather connect to My power to provide for you and sustain you. It is in My loving arms that I give you clarity of mind as I shine light and truth to lies, wrong thinking and negative and deceiving thoughts that you have been believing. My child, come to Me in the wilderness so I can walk with you through to the Promised Land.

The desert and the parched land will be glad; the wilderness will rejoice and blossom. Like the crocus, it will burst into bloom; it will rejoice greatly and shout for joy. The glory of Lebanon will be given to it, the splendor of Carmel and Sharon; they will see the glory of the Lord, the splendor of our God.
—Isaiah 35:1-2

NOVEMBER 23

$\mathscr{F}$aith is your victory. It is the goal you want to work toward. Faith is trusting in Me and believing what I say is true. It's trusting in My promises. It is knowing that when you have no clue what to do, I do know and will show you. It is when you are concerned about someone's safety, you rest in peace knowing I'm in control. It's when a crisis suddenly appears, you do not fear but turn to Me. It is knowing with full confidence that I am here. Ask Me for faith. May faith be what stays rooted in your thoughts rather than doubt or fear. How freeing that will be for you! Oh, My child, won't you make this your goal?

Now faith is confidence in what we hope for and assurance about what we do not see. By faith Noah, when warned about things not yet seen, in holy fear built an ark to save his family. By his faith he condemned the world and became heir of the righteousness that is in keeping with faith.
—Hebrews 11:1,7

NOVEMBER 24

$\mathscr{T}$hanksgiving Day is the day set aside to purposefully look at all My blessings I've given you and to be grateful. I want you to give thanks in everything, for this is My will for you. It is so easy to be thankful for the good things, but I also want you to give thanks for the things that you consider not so good. I know you may be questioning this instruction and wonder how you can possibly give thanks. The answer is you can't, unless you recognize that I allow things in your life for My good purposes and glory. Joseph is an example of this truth that I want you to follow. His jealous brothers sold him into slavery and he was imprisoned under false charges, but I used this difficult situation to save the lives of many people, including these brothers. Learn from this example and make the conscious decision to choose gratitude instead of bitterness, anger or blame. By making this choice, you are acknowledging that I am good even when circumstances are not, and you will have peace.

And now, do not be distressed and do not be angry with yourselves for selling me here, because it was to save lives that God sent me ahead of you. He made me father to Pharaoh, lord of his entire household and ruler of all Egypt. You intended to harm me, but God intended it for good to accomplish what is now being done, the saving of many lives.
—Genesis 45:5, 8b, 50:20

Rejoice always, pray continually, give thanks in all circumstances;
for this is God's will for you in Christ Jesus. —1 Thessalonians 5:16-18

*S*ometimes you focus on what should have been or could have been. Please train yourself not to dwell on that kind of thinking. They are thoughts that focus on the past and keep your attention on what you don't have or can't have. Joy can't be attained with this kind of thinking. Rather, focus on the present, even if it is not how you want it to be. Refocus on what you DO have. One by one, thank Me for these things! Think about how I have not left your side! Look for how I am working everything for good. Peace, contentment and joy can only be found in this way of thinking.

A cheerful heart is good medicine, but a crushed spirit dries up the bones.
—Proverbs 17:22

Finally, brothers, whatever is true, whatever is honorable, whatever is just, whatever is pure, whatever is lovely, whatever is commendable, if there is any excellence, if there is anything worthy of praise, think about these things.
—Philippians 4:8 (ESV)

*M*y greatest gift to you is My love. It is a pure love, focused only on you, and that is freely given and unconditional. It is a faithful, committed and persistent love. You can't escape My love. It is ever-pursuing even when you walk in disobedience; I love you with all that I am. My Son would have given His life even if it was just for you. Focus your attention on knowing, feeling and sensing My love. I want to touch your wounded and weary heart. I want to penetrate your hardened heart, the part that is closed off to Me, that you want to continue to control. I am not condemning you; I just want all of you. That is My heart's desire. I want to overwhelm you with this love and as you allow yourself to experience it totally, your life will never be the same.

But God demonstrates his own love for us in this: While we were still sinners, Christ died for us.
—Romans 5:8

And I pray that you, being rooted and established in love, may have power, together with all the Lord's holy people, to grasp how wide and long and high and deep is the love of Christ, and to know this love that surpasses knowledge— that you may be filled to the measure of all the fullness of God.
—Ephesians 3:17b-19

*J*want you to become everything I created you to be. That is of great importance to Me. I lovingly stretch you, mature you and bring you to a place of maximum potential out of My love for you as your Father. I do this through discipline that sometimes brings about My loving rod of correction. Please understand it is correction, not punishment, and it is never done in anger towards you. It is done in love and seeing and wanting your potential to be realized. I want you to share in My holiness. It may be painful at times, but I am right by your side, encouraging you, strengthening you and cheering you on! In the end, it will produce righteousness and peace and will draw you closer to Me.

My son, do not despise the Lord's discipline, and do not resent his rebuke,
because the Lord disciplines those he loves, as a father the son he delights in.
—Proverbs 3:11-12

God disciplines us for our good, in order that we may share in his holiness.
No discipline seems pleasant at the time, but painful. Later on, however, it produces
a harvest of righteousness and peace for those who have been trained by it.
—Hebrews 12:10b-11

*M*y heart's desire is that you become totally dependent on Me. This goes against everything the world says and believes. I know you do give Me your problems, but then you take them right back again, sometimes without even realizing it. You do this because subconsciously you trust yourself more than you trust Me. I am not saying this to bring condemnation but to help you see a better way. If you are honest with yourself, you think it is difficult to trust Me completely with your life and to give Me total control. It is only as you draw closer to Me and spend time getting to know My heart through My Word that your faith will begin to rise as you start to place your trust in a Father that you truly know. I am aware of your struggles and wait with open arms for you to come to Me in total surrender. My heart is for you to experience My peace and joy every day, no matter what you are going through. My heart is for you to live your life consciously aware of My power and love flowing through you. Won't you give Me My heart's desire?

"But blessed is the one who trusts in the Lord, whose confidence is in him. They will be like a tree
planted by the water that sends out its roots by the stream. It does not fear when heat comes; its
leaves are always green. It has no worries in a year of drought and never fails to bear fruit."
—Jeremiah 17:7-8

*P*eace eludes you My child. The peace I have for you and want to give you is what you run away from, and you're not even aware of it. You seek peace in the wrong places. I am not sharing this to make you feel bad but because I care about you. It breaks My heart to see you struggle like this. The world's solution for peace is fleeting and not genuine. Come to Me. Bring Me all your concerns and frustrations and let Me handle them. Trust that I know the whole picture and what is best for you, and that I am a bigger God than your problems. My peace is real and long-lasting if you embrace it. Come, My child and choose the better way.

Peace I leave with you; my peace I give you. I do not give to you as the world gives. Do not let your hearts be troubled and do not be afraid. —John 14:27

You keep him in perfect peace whose mind is stayed on you, because he trusts in you. —Isaiah 26:3 (ESV)

*W*hen you came to know Me, I came to live in you in the form of the Holy Spirit. The Spirit is the least known of the Trinity. You are familiar with Me and My Son, but the Holy Spirit sometimes remains a mystery. Let Me share with you who The Spirit is. He is a divine person because He has a mind, emotions and a will. He tells your heart the truth about Me and reveals My will to you. He searches all things and knows My thoughts and illuminates the truth in you. The Spirit determines the spiritual gifts you have as a believer and guides you in discovering and using them. He lives in you to produce My character in your life and helps you to display the fruit of the Holy Spirit. On your own strength, you can't show love, joy, peace, patience, kindness, goodness, faithfulness, gentleness and self-control, but the Holy Spirit empowers you. He also works in the lives of unbelievers, convicting their hearts of My truths and nudging them to repent and turn to Me for forgiveness and a new life. Spend time connecting with My Spirit living in you.

What we have received is not the spirit of the world, but the Spirit who is from God, so that we may understand what God has freely given us. —1 Corinthians 2:12

In the same way, the Spirit helps us in our weakness. We do not know what we ought to pray for, but the Spirit himself intercedes for us through wordless groans. And he who searches our hearts knows the mind of the Spirit, because the Spirit intercedes for God's people in accordance with the will of God. —Romans 8:26-27

DECEMBER 1

You want so much to believe in Me and walk in faith. I honor your heart's intention. Sometimes you are walking in faith and have peace, but there are other times where you have missed the mark. I want to reveal this to you to prevent the frustration, uncertainty and fear you have when this happens. You ask Me to show you My will and then you come up with a plan. It is a good plan, even a godly plan, but sometimes it is not My plan. Even though your intentions are good, what you are really doing is trusting Me to support your plan which will not give you peace or assurance. Sometimes My timing may frustrate you also, but walk in faith, knowing I am never late and I will show you the way. When you are following My will, you will walk in faith, totally assured that everything will work out even while walking the unknown.

So faith comes from hearing, and hearing through the word of Christ.
—Romans 10:17 (ESV)

Therefore we are always confident and know that as long as we are at home in the body we are away from the Lord. For we live by faith, not by sight.
—2 Corinthians 5:6-7

DECEMBER 2

You find yourself complaining about a situation you are in. Sometimes it is grumbling about the same thing over and over again. You think to yourself, "I'm not complaining. I'm just stating the facts." or "I'm only giving my opinion and telling it like it is." My child, I lovingly say to you that is wrong thinking. These negative thoughts are not from Me. That is not My character. I detest grumbling. When you complain, you aren't connected to Me or My Lordship over your life. Self-centeredness has taken over as well as unbelief in what I can do. Let grumbling become an indicator, and when you become aware of it, reconnect to Me, allowing My peace and joy to flow through you. Won't you try the better way?

Do everything without grumbling or arguing, so that you may become blameless and pure, "children of God without fault in a warped and crooked generation." Then you will shine among them like stars in the sky.
—Philippians 2:14-15

Do not let any unwholesome talk come out of your mouths, but only what is helpful for building others up according to their needs, that it may benefit those who listen.
—Ephesians 4:29

DECEMBER 3

$\mathcal{A}$s you go about your day and are mingling with others, you are constantly observing them whether you are aware of it or not. Observing how people look and act is not a sin, but when you put judgment to it, you cross the line. You think to yourself that they're showing a lot of skin, or they are conceited, insecure, self-centered, or not doing things the way you would. You think they're really crude, overweight, obnoxious or mean-spirited. Sometimes you're not even aware that you are thinking these things or that it is judging and is a sin in My eyes. Instead of judging what you see, ask Me to show you what I see, for I see the big picture. I see the broken home life, abuse, their deep hurts and disappointments, their wrong thinking and lies that they are believing. I see their discouragement and sense of unworthiness and hopelessness. If only they knew that My Son died to set them free. I see they need compassion, understanding and most of all, My love! Will you see what I see and love them instead of judging?

There is only one lawgiver and judge, he who is able to save and to destroy. But who are you to judge your neighbor? —James 4:12 (ESV)

Stop judging by mere appearances, but instead judge correctly. —John 7:24

DECEMBER 4

$\mathcal{Y}$ou anticipate being in a situation you do not want to be in. It involves having to be at the same function as someone who has hurt you deeply or who is living life in a way that you know is wrong. You do not want to be in the same room, much less have to acknowledge their presence. Everything about it makes you sick and you are full of dread. You fight your inner feelings of wanting to speak your mind and being unkind. Stop a moment and realize these thoughts are not from Me. Refocus your thoughts on what will give you peace. You are My child and My Holy Spirit lives in you. Let Me be the sole judge and let your judgment go. Access My love, kindness, goodness and self-control; then step out of the way and allow Me to work in you. They may have sinned, but, My child, you do too. Show them My heart. Even if you say or do nothing, your heart is changed and it will show. Go forth filled with My love, light and power and pour into those who need to experience Me. I won't leave your side.

For the Spirit God gave us does not make us timid, but gives us power, love and self-discipline. —2 Timothy 1:7

For I am the Lord your God who takes hold of your right hand and says to you, Do not fear; I will help you. —Isaiah 41:13 NIV

DECEMBER 5

When you are going through a difficult storm in your life, know that I am there with you. The timing for seeing results may not be your timing, but it is the perfect time. When you need Me the most and waiver in your hope, I am there for you. I come in unexpected and unfamiliar ways. Sometimes you question this but I have a purpose in all of My ways, for I am looking at your heart. Are you focusing on Me or following your own heart and what you want to see happen? This may seem harsh to you, but, My child, I do it for you, to teach you skills and build your character. When the next storm comes, you will be better equipped to handle it, resting in My peace.

God is our refuge and strength, an ever-present help in trouble.
—Psalm 46:1

He caused the storm to be still, so that the waves of the sea were hushed.
—Psalm 107:29 (NASB)

DECEMBER 6

You sometimes wonder how I can use you for My Kingdom's work with all the flaws you see in yourself and things you've done that were wrong. Even though you've asked for forgiveness, you realize you still mess up every day. Sometimes this is preventing you from realizing your full potential that I have in store for you. Look in the Old Testament at My servant David. He sinned by committing adultery and ordered the murder of an innocent man to cover it up. When confronted with his sin, he genuinely repented. He did have to face the consequences of these sins, but he kept his focus on Me to see him through. My grace was there for him, and restoration and healing took place. He was used mightily by Me, and I called him a man after My own heart because that is who he became. Look to this example when you feel discouraged. My heart is to see lives redeemed. I rejoice with all of heaven when this happens.

After removing Saul, he made David their king. God testified concerning him: 'I have found David son of Jesse, a man after my own heart; he will do everything I want him to do.'
—Acts 13:22

I tell you that in the same way there will be more rejoicing in heaven over one sinner who repents than over ninety-nine righteous persons who do not need to repent.
—Luke 15:7 NIV

I am your protector and defender. I deliver you from the hands of the wicked. No matter what you are facing, I am bigger than it is. I am all powerful, for there is no one and no thing with more power! I am a protective Father and I always shield My children. Knowing this truth will give you peace and rest in your soul. May it give you confidence that I am your refuge and fortress. Think on these truths when faced with opposition. I am your source of peace.

In you, Lord, I have taken refuge; let me never be put to shame. In your righteousness, rescue me and deliver me; turn your ear to me and save me. Be my rock of refuge, to which I can always go; give the command to save me, for you are my rock and my fortress. Deliver me, my God, from the hand of the wicked, from the grasp of those who are evil and cruel.
—Psalm 71:1-4

*Y*ou look at your life and realize the path that you took was clearly the wrong one, and now you find your life in a total mess. You have remorse and feel discouraged and hopeless. You don't know what to do and just want to give up or run away. My child, My heart goes out to you. I value your life and see the potential. Even when you mess up big time, that does not mean it is the end of anything good coming out of your life. My Son died for this very reason, to redeem your life. It is My heart that all My creation be redeemed. Come, repent and confess your sins; turn away from them and turn to Me. Seek Me and My ways and I will help you in this transition and new beginning. I will encourage you and give you everything you need to follow Me if you allow Me to. I will call out your potential and destiny in Me and help you in rebuilding your life—a life redeemed in Me. This is a new day and a new beginning! Won't you come and turn to Me?

For he has rescued us from the dominion of darkness and brought us into the kingdom of the Son he loves, in whom we have redemption, the forgiveness of sins.
—Colossians 1:13-14

In him we have redemption through his blood, the forgiveness of sins, in accordance with the riches of God's grace.
—Ephesians 1:7

DECEMBER 9

*T*here's a battle going on for your very soul. Satan tugs at you with lies and deception that seem so plausible and real. Without you even knowing it, he will ensnare you with thoughts that there's no way out of this, that it can't get better, that the doctors are right, or that you can't do this. You feel like you're in a dark pit with no way out. But if you take your eyes off of the lies, you will see it's not a deep pit after all and you can easily climb out. You will also see I am right there waiting patiently for you to come to Me. I won't ever force you like the enemy does, but I stand by your side with loving arms extended, ready to embrace you when you turn your eyes to Me. When I am your focus, your thoughts become centered on possibilities and hope.

Jesus replied, "What is impossible with man is possible with God."
—Luke 18:27

For I know the plans that I have for you, says the Lord,
plans for peace and not for evil, to give you a future and a hope.
—Jeremiah 29:11 (MEV)

DECEMBER 10

*T*here are occasions in your life where you want to "fast forward" time. You may be looking forward to a vacation or Christmas and wish it were here now. You may be counting down the days until you can retire, until a mortgage is paid off, until you get the test results back, or until a difficult situation you are in will pass. Oh My child, I understand you want these things to come sooner, but please don't wish time away. I want you to change your way of thinking. Each day is a gift I give to you and an opportunity to enjoy the blessings I have for you. Stop and look for My goodness in each day, in the ways you see My hand upon your life. Find the beauty of today and relish the moment. Even when you are going through difficult circumstances, look for the ways I am watching out for you and walking by your side, and appreciate them with Me. Please don't waste any seconds of the time I have given you, but find their worth. You will notice the difference this change will make in you.

This is the day that the Lord has made; let us rejoice and be glad in it.
—Psalm 118:24 (ESV)

But godliness with contentment is great gain. For we brought nothing into the world, and we can take nothing out of it. But if we have food and clothing, we will be content with that.
—1 Timothy 6:6-8

*W*ho has control over your mind? Are you believing thoughts that make you feel worthless, insecure, fearful, guilty, or ashamed? Are your thoughts making you feel dread, anger, distrust, resentment, or temptation? Oh, My child, these thoughts are not from Me. Satan is doing everything he can to bring you down, to disrupt your life and to rob you of all joy, peace and contentment. He's trying to demean and demoralize you, to make you start to question yourself and to wear you down. He's doing everything he can to keep you from Me, including telling you that I am a mean, judgmental God. Please stop believing these lies. Choose My truth instead. What you can count on is that I love you and will not give up on you ever. I am always by your side and will never leave you alone. I want to fill you with hope and peace and to give you all the things a loving Father gives to His beloved child. Please won't you choose to fill your mind with all of My goodness that I have for you?

The coming of the lawless one will be in accordance with how Satan works. He will us all sorts of displays of power through signs and wonders that serve the lie, and all the ways that wickedness deceives those who are perishing. They perish because they refused to love the truth and so be saved. —2 Thessalonians 2:9-10

But I am afraid that just as Eve was deceived by the serpent's cunning, your minds may somehow be led astray from your sincere and pure devotion to Christ. —2 Corinthians 11:3

*P*rayer is powerful. Instead of taking pain medicine when you have a headache, make prayer your first course of action. Do not discount its effectiveness. Heaven and earth are literally moved by prayer. When you pray with all concerns laid aside and tune into My will, the heavens open and My glory is displayed. Pray without ceasing. Stay prayed and praised up so that, when a situation arises, the faith is already there. You're already connected and you will see what I'm doing. Walk in this atmosphere as much as you can and watch Me work!

Therefore I tell you, whatever you ask for in prayer, believe that you have received it, and it will be yours. —Mark 11:24

This is the confidence we have in approaching God: that if we as anything according to his will, he hears us. And if we know that he hears us—whatever we ask—we know that we have what we asked of him. —1 John 5:14-15

*Y*ou've been offended by someone and are harboring anger, resentment and bitterness. You think about what happened and repeat it over and over again in your mind. Oh My child, don't stay there, for it will only eat away at you. Don't give the devil a foothold. I want to speak to your heart. It's not always as it seems. You aren't seeing the heart of the person that offended you. You don't see their pain, fear, or the lies they are believing. If you knew, it would help you understand that their actions came out of brokenness, even if they were wrong. Sometimes what you perceive to have taken place wasn't totally accurate; it's your perception of reality. Sometimes when you replay the offending scene in your mind, you add things to it that weren't a part of it. These are all dynamics that you aren't even aware of. Please choose to let go of the offense for your own sake so you can have peace again and the devil doesn't have his way with you. Choose to forgive the person, which doesn't mean you will forget it happened, but you forgive because it is My will for you and the only way to stop the inner turmoil you feel. Choose to stop thinking about the offense and even begin to pray for that person. Watch how that changes your attitude. When you begin to make these choices, it will give you the peace you are seeking and will set you free.

Good sense makes one slow to anger, and it is his glory to overlook an offense.
—Proverbs 19:11 (ESV)

If you are angry, don't sin by nursing your grudge. Don't let the sun go down with you still angry—get over it quickly; for when you are angry, you give a mighty foothold to the devil.
—Ephesians 4:26-27 (TLB)

*Y*ou hold back at times from sharing about Me with others. You want to keep this spiritual part of your life to yourself because you think this should be private. Where are you getting these thoughts, My child? They aren't from Me. Satan wants to silence your mouth, but that is not My plan. I want you to open up to others when there is an opportunity. Share with them what I mean to you and how I have worked in your life. Simply share from your heart; that's all I ask of you. I will empower you and give you boldness and the words to say. Share the Good News and I will do the rest by touching their hearts. You never know how your act of obedience can impact a person's life.

He said to them, "Go into all the world and preach the gospel to all creation. Whoever believes and is baptized will be saved, but whoever does not believe will be condemned."
—Mark 16:15-16

Declare his glory among the nations, his marvelous deeds among all peoples.
—Psalm 96:3

I want you to find the wonder in encountering Me. Your wonder has been lost, as has the fresh excitement and awe of anticipating and being in My presence. You have slowly allowed the problems of life to consume you, and it grieves My heart to see you this way. I want you to regain the fresh wonder of being in My presence and have this consume you instead. Come, sit down, quiet yourself and open up your imagination. Tune in to My presence all around you. Experience heaven right here on earth, for it can be done. I want to reveal Myself to you in ways you haven't experienced yet. Be still before Me and wait with anticipation. Tell Me. "What do you see? What are you hearing? What can you smell or taste? What are you feeling? Be patient if you feel you aren't receiving anything. Persevering is part of the marvelous journey. Keep on pressing in. Take your time and experience My glory!

Let all the earth fear the Lord; let all the inhabitants of the world stand in awe of him!
—Psalm 33:8 (ESV)

When Jacob awoke from his sleep, he thought, "Surely the Lord is in this place, and I was not aware of it." He was afraid and said, "How awesome is this place! This is none other than the house of God; this is the gate of heaven."
—Genesis 28:16-17

*Y*ou feel as if what you are facing is overwhelming and impossible to achieve. You doubt your ability to do anything about the situation and feel like quitting or running away. My child, this may be hard for you to understand, but sometimes I allow these challenges you face. You might wonder why a loving father would do such a thing. It is because I am a loving Father that I sometimes need to get your attention. It's easy to trust Me when everything is going well, but that won't help you cope when things don't go well. It is through facing difficulties that your faith will be strengthened. I sometimes remove false securities and feelings of contentment so that you look to Me for your source of strength and direction. Look at My servant Gideon who learned to place his full trust in Me when I had him whittle down his powerful army of 32,000 to just 300 men to fight the vast powerful enemy before them. He learned that he could not have victory without Me being in control. You may have suffered a tremendous loss or are facing something very serious, but undoing these things is not what you need to win the battle you face. I have not abandoned you nor will I ever! Stand firm in Me with your focus on what I can do in and for you. With everything that gave you a false sense of security removed, you will be amazed, like Gideon, at what I can achieve through you! Put your trust in Me.

The Lord turned to him and said, "Go in the strength you have and save Israel out of Midian's hand. Am I not sending you?" "Pardon me, my lord," Gideon replied, "but how can I save Israel? My clan is the weakest in Manasseh, and I am the least in my family." The Lord answered, "I will be with you, and you will strike down all the Midianites, leaving none alive." The Lord said to Gideon, "You have too many men. I cannot deliver Midian into their hands, or Israel would boast against me, 'My own strength has saved me.'" The Lord said to Gideon, "With the three hundred men that lapped I will save you and give the Midianites into your hands. Let all the others go home."

—Judges 6:14-16, 7:2,7

DECEMBER 17

*W*hat do you fear? Is it being alone, running out of money, the dark, getting sick or dying, or the unknown? Some fears you don't even realize you have, but it keeps you from reaching your potential. Other fears are paralyzing. How many of your fears ever came to fruition? Fear does not come from Me but is Satan's tactic to deprive you of your peace and joy. As soon as you're aware of the fear, give it to Me and trust that I will see you through the situation. Make that decision and don't hang on to the fear. Please realize I am with you no matter what comes your way in life. My perfect love casts out all fear. When you are connected to Me, you're focused on My glory, goodness and power and fear vanishes in My presence. Keep your thoughts on Me and who I am to you.

Now may the Lord of peace himself give you peace at all times and in every way. The Lord be with all of you. —2 Thessalonians 3:16

The Lord is my light and my salvation—whom shall I fear? The Lord is the stronghold of my life—of whom shall I be afraid? —Psalm 27:1 NIV

DECEMBER 18

*W*eep for the lost. Won't you weep with Me? I will give you eyes to see what I see, which is the brokenness of mankind. They do things that are hurtful, immoral, selfish and wrong, and they don't even know it or care. They are so broken and ensnared by sin. Join Me in loving them, praying for them and even reaching out to them. Don't give up on them or judge. They are the lost sheep that need to find their way home to Me.

What do you think? If a man has a hundred sheep, and one of them has gone astray, does he not leave the ninety-nine on the mountains and go in search of the one that went astray? And if he finds it, truly, I say to you, he rejoices over it more than over the ninety-nine that never went astray. So it is not the will of my Father who is in heaven that one of these little ones should perish. —Matthew 18:12-14 (ESV)

My brothers and sisters, if one of you should wander from the truth and someone should bring that person back, remember this: Whoever turns a sinner from the error of their way will save them from death and cover over a multitude of sins. —James 5:19-20

*Y*ou find yourself overwhelmed and stressed, and there's a feeling of torment and gloom hanging over you. As hard as you try, you can't seem to get rid of these feelings even though you are trying to connect to Me. You give Me your problems and then, without thinking, you pick them up again and go back to thinking about the situation you are in that is causing these feelings. You try to be still before Me, but your mind keeps racing, and you don't know how to turn it off. My child, as much as I want to help you, I can't when you allow these thoughts to fill your mind. I don't mean to discourage you, but I can't work in your life when these thoughts are consuming you. You have to be the one to choose My peace. Try again, My dear one and keep trying. Know I am right there with you, cheering you on. Choose right now to be still before Me. Quiet your mind. Take every negative thought captive. Don't let Satan win this war. It may be hard work, but you can do it; I give you the strength if you allow Me. Feel My peace flowing through you. Stay in that moment and hold on to that peace. You hold that peace by realizing I will fight your battle while you watch from a place of rest. Once you allow Me to fill your mind, I can work in your life. Persevere so that My presence fills your thoughts and you find the peace that you are seeking. I am with you, My child. I want so much for you to experience My perfect peace.

But I see another law at work in me, waging war against the law of my mind and making me a prisoner of the law of sin at work within me.
—Romans 7:23

You keep him in perfect peace whose mind is stayed on you, because he trusts in you.
—Isaiah 26:3 (ESV)

DECEMBER 20

I am a just God. My heart is to see all mankind spend eternity with Me, and I went to great lengths for that to happen. My Son took on all of man's sin on the cross and willingly died so all may live eternally with Me. I love all of My creation equally, and I give each one a free will to make their own choices. The only way for you to be with Me in heaven is through belief in My Son, Jesus. Please don't believe the lie that being a good person or doing good things will get you into heaven. Salvation is a free gift and you can't do anything to earn it. Please share this truth with anyone you come in contact with who believes differently. I will give you the words; just share from your heart. You may be the person who helps them change their future destiny. My heart's desire is for all to enter My Heavenly Kingdom, but it is a choice everyone must make on their own.

For God so loved the world that he gave his one and only Son,
that whoever believes in him shall not perish but have eternal life.   —John 3:16

Jesus answered, "I am the way and the truth and the life.
No one comes to the Father except through me."   —John 14:6

DECEMBER 21

S ometimes you struggle with feeling inadequate to do My work or just with life in general. You feel as if you aren't good, smart, or worthy enough, or that you are un-qualified or lack enough experience. You may feel as if your past failures are holding you back. Those are all lies from the enemy. Remember your identity is in Me. I have equipped you with everything you need for life and godliness. Let go of all negative thoughts and inadequacies, and exchange them for your identity in Me and your destiny. Recall how Moses gave Me excuses for why he couldn't do what I called him to do, but after he yielded, I used him mightily. I want to use you mightily too!

Not that we are competent in ourselves to claim anything
for ourselves, but our competence comes from God.   —2 Corinthians 3:5

"So now, go. I am sending you to Pharaoh to bring my people the Israelites out of Egypt." But
Moses said to God, "Who am I that I should go to Pharaoh and bring the Israelites out of Egypt?"
And God said, "I will be with you. And this will be the sign to you that it is I who have sent you:
When you have brought the people out of Egypt, you will worship God on this mountain."
—Exodus 3:10-12

DECEMBER 22

*T*his nation is coming to a critical juncture in time. No more is it defined by its Christianity but by its trying to please and include everyone for love's sake. My heart is breaking for this nation. I watch as My Word is slowly getting reinterpreted, succumbing to vocal opponents' opinions. The deceiving lies are ensnaring many. Be on guard. Do not entertain any thought that is not from My Word. You may struggle with this as the world's ways are ever present in our lives and can be so inviting and may seem so right in your eyes. I do implore you to love all mankind as I do and not to judge anyone, for that is My role alone. That does not change My Word though, for I am very clear in what is not pleasing to Me. Your role is to love as I love but also uphold My Word as truth. Do not waiver. Stand strong and be bold in Me.

For the time will come when people will not put up with sound doctrine. Instead, to suit their own desires, they will gather around them a great number of teachers to say what their itching ears want to hear. They will turn their ears away from the truth and turn aside to myths. But you, keep your head in all situations, endure hardship, do the work of an evangelist, discharge all the duties of your ministry.

—2 Timothy 4:3-5

If my people, who are called by my name, will humble themselves and pray and seek my face and turn from their wicked ways, then I will hear from heaven, and I will forgive their sin and will heal their land.

—II Chronicles 7:14

I want you to come to Me in total surrender, laying down control of your life and everything you're holding on to. My heart's desire for you is to allow Me to be Lord of your life and every aspect of it. Why do you hesitate? I don't want you to feel bad, but My heart breaks with knowing everything I want to give you if only you would let go of what is preventing you from the riches I have for you. Worries, stress, guilt, or restlessness don't have to be a part of your life. Take one step at a time, letting go of your fear, pride, control and doubt. Each step you take in letting go brings you one step closer to My presence, adds to your knowledge of who I am and increases your faith. Keep your focus on Me with each new step and do not waiver or look back. As you get closer, My presence becomes bigger in your mind and your problems and baggage become smaller. Each step of surrendering gives you more confidence that you're not missing what you let go of because what you're receiving from Me is so much better. Living from My peace, contentment and joy replaces the old negative feelings you lived with. As you draw closer to My presence and let go of additional baggage, you begin to forget about it all; as you gaze into My eyes and realize everything I said, all My promises are true and real. As you step closer in this process, you feel My love, power, safety and peace more intensely. It will transform your life. Won't you allow Me to give you these riches I have for you?

The Lord will guide you always; he will satisfy your needs in a sun-scorched land and will strengthen your frame. You will be like a well-watered garden, like a spring whose waters never fail.

—Isaiah 58:11

Every good and perfect gift is from above, coming down from the Father of the heavenly lights, who does not change like shifting shadows.

—James 1:17

Christmas Eve

*D*uring this Christmas season, focus on what My Son was born to give you. While the world focuses on bargains and buying, I have given you a role model to emulate. Your focus, especially this month, is on a baby being born in humble surroundings, who walked in humility and who showed My love and compassion to everyone. Jesus was born with a purpose, to follow My plan. He was born to show you who I really am and to reveal to you My nature and character. He was the ultimate role model for you— to teach you how to live out your lives in a way pleasing to Me. Most importantly, Jesus was born to bring you into a full intimate relationship with Me, the Father He knew so well. Follow His example and make it a priority to seek My presence and communicate with Me throughout your day. Jesus also came to give you assurance of life with Me forever and also life with abundance for the present. As you get caught up in Christmas preparations, pause, and don't lose sight of whom the focus should be on. No Christmas present you will open this month compares to this most precious gift of all!

For to us a child is born, to us a son is given, and the government will be on his shoulders. And he will be called Wonderful Counselor, Mighty God, Everlasting Father, Prince of Peace. Of the greatness of his government and peace there will be no end. He will reign on David's throne and over his kingdom, establishing and upholding it with justice and righteousness from that time on and forever.
—Isaiah 9:6-7a

"She will give birth to a son, and you are to give him the name Jesus, because he will save his people from their sins." "The virgin will conceive and give birth to a son, and they will call him Immanuel, which means God with us".
—Matthew 1:21, 23

DECEMBER 25

Christmas Day

*T*oday you will celebrate the birth of My Son, Jesus, My precious gift to you! I want you to celebrate more than that He was just a baby being born, but what this gift means to you as you live out your daily life. His birth gives you access to eternal life in the future and abundant life for right now. Because of Jesus, you can experience peace that passes your understanding no matter what you are going through. You can learn to feel My power and strength in you when you are falling apart. You can feel My presence when you need to be comforted. Because of Jesus, your path is lit before you when you are faced with difficult decisions. When you don't know how to make ends meet, My provision is there. Because of Jesus, you are comforted when you are overwhelmed. You are healed and restored. You have hope and encouragement when you don't see the way out. You now have access to My refreshing touch and My joy no matter what you are facing. Come, celebrate Jesus' birth!

Today in the town of David a Savior has been born to you; he is the Messiah, the Lord.
—Luke 2:11

Thanks be to God for his indescribable gift!   —2 Corinthians 9:15

DECEMBER 26

*T*here are gifts all around you that I have given you which sadly haven't been opened. There is no condemnation, but I want you to become aware of this. No matter where you are in your relationship with Me, I have so much more to share with you. I want you to experience more and more of My goodness. Seek after these things and actively pursue them. Ask Me for help. There are other gifts for you, too, that you aren't accessing; and as a result you find yourself discouraged, stressed, full of fear or worry. It is My intent for you to experience peace, contentment and joy in all things. That sounds daunting to you, but this is part of the gifts that I will help you open and show you how to use.

May the God of hope fill you with all joy and peace as you trust in him,
so that you may overflow with hope by the power of the Holy Spirit. —Romans 15:13

Consider it pure joy, my brothers and sisters, whenever you face trials of many kinds,
because you know that the testing of your faith produces perseverance. Let perseverance
finish its work so that you may be mature and complete, not lacking anything.
—James 1:2-4

𝒴our life is filled with work, family, commitments, chores and activities. Finding time for yourself or taking care of yourself is low on your priority list. You also have trouble making the time to spend with Me, and that bothers you. You're torn between keeping up with everything you do and knowing deep down it's just not working. Every day you live with stress, frustration and feel overwhelmed. You see people all around you taking pills or coping in other ways that are just not healthy. You don't see the end in sight and you question how you can continue. My child, My heart feels your pain, for this is not how I intended your life or other people's lives to be. I know everything you do is important in your mind, but your health is of great importance to Me. I want you to take a close look at all the things you do and see what you can give up, lay aside for a season, or delegate to others. Let go of wanting everything to be perfect, for that is a lie you are believing and that is not what is important to Me. I will gladly guide you in this process and show you My will if you just ask Me. I will even take away your desire for perfection and holding on to things that I want you to lay aside. I will give you strength and sustain you for the things that you need to keep doing and that are in My will. My child, let Me help you find the peace that you are yearning for.

"Come to me, all you who are weary and burdened, and I will give you rest. Take my yoke upon you and learn from me, for I am gentle and humble in heart, and you will find rest for your souls. For my yoke is easy and my burden is light."
—Matthew 11:28-30

Peace I leave with you; my peace I give you. I do not give to you as the world gives. Do not let your hearts be troubled and do not be afraid.
—John 14:27

*Y*ou pray, read your Bible, worship Me and do all sorts of things in My name. All are pleasing and of great value to Me. But I am calling you to learn to be still and abide in Me. Being still means not praying or praising but quieting your mind and soul before Me. It means resting and being filled with My glory, power and love and allowing Me to work in you. If you aren't feeling anything, don't be concerned for I see the difference already taking place. As you learn to quiet your mind and abide in Me, your trust in Me will quicken—even when you don't understand everything or in spite of going through tough times. You trust and rest in My promises and your belief deepens of who I say I am to you. You are quicker to recognize and reject the enemy's lies. You learn to see what I see as I reveal this to you. You begin to give Me more and more control of your life as you surrender it to a Father you know personally. Being still before Me is a process and will probably be hard to do initially. Keep persevering, for the rewards are great.

Remain in me, as I also remain in you. No branch can bear fruit by itself; it must remain in the vine. Neither can you bear fruit unless you remain in me. —John 15:4

I have been crucified with Christ and I no longer live, but Christ lives in me. The life I now live in the body, I live by faith in the Son of God, who loved me and gave himself for me.
—Galatians 2:20

DECEMBER 29

*M*y heart is for you to be content, to feel peace and to experience joy. All three of these are attainable in any situation you are in. Paul learned how to do this and experienced it while chained in a cell. The secret is quite simple. Pray continually, keeping Me in focus rather than the problem. Give thanks in all circumstances and cultivate a grateful heart which is always looking for something to be thankful for. Learn to rejoice always; purposely look for something to be joyful about in whatever you face. In each of these, your attention is directed to something positive and where I am. Look for My goodness in all things.

Rejoice always, pray continually, give thanks in all circumstances; for this is God's will for you in Christ Jesus.
—1 Thessalonians 5:16-18

I have learned the secret of being content in any and every situation, whether well fed or hungry, whether living in plenty or in want.
—Philippians 4:12b

DECEMBER 30

*A*t this time every year, you think about what your New Year's resolution is. And every year not too long afterwards, the resolution becomes a distant memory. You often wonder what happened because you had such good intentions. Often you are relying on your own strength which doesn't last. You may also be relying on what you think is a good resolution rather than asking Me. Let Me show you a better way! When you begin to think about what your resolution should be, ask Me first what My will is for you. If you are seeking Me with all of your heart, you won't need anything else because everything then comes out of the relationship you have with Me. Make Me your first priority, for I equip you with everything you need to follow through. Watch the difference this will make and how I will work in your life this coming year!

Now may the God of peace, equip you with everything good for doing his will,
and may he work in us what is pleasing to him, through Jesus Christ.
—Hebrews 13:20a-2a

For everything in the world—the lust of the flesh, the lust of the eyes,
and the pride of life—comes not from the Father but from the world. The world
and its desires pass away, but whoever does the will of God lives forever.
—1 John 2:16-17

DECEMBER 31

I love that you spent this year with Me getting to know Me better and learning My ways. I love that your heart is teachable and that you are willing to step out of your comfort zone to explore the better way. You've gotten to know My heart and slowly your heart is melding with Mine, which gives Me great delight. I know you yearn for more and that peace sometimes eludes you, but it is attainable. Continue on this journey with Me and walk in My peace.

Peace I leave with you; peace I give you. I do not give to you as the
world gives. Do not let your hearts be troubled and do not be afraid.
—John 14:27

"And surely I am with you always, to the very end of the age."
—Matthew 28:20b

Topical Reference

Abundant Life Mar 1, 29; Apr 3; June 13, 23; July 5; Aug 1, 10, 23; Sept 11; Oct 24, 29

Almighty God May 27; Sept 26; Nov 11

Alone Jan 14, 17; Feb 27; Mar 3; Sept 26; Oct 17, 23

Anger Feb 20, 23; Apr 8; May 31; June 30; July 17; Aug 9, 27; Dec 13

Battlefield Of The Mind Dec 19

Be Still Jan 4, 26; Apr 16; Sept 29; Oct 19; Nov 10; Dec 28

Betrayal July 30

Bible Jan 28, 29; May 12, 13; July 10; Aug 21; Sept 5, 17; Oct 25

Bitterness Feb 20, 23; May 31; June 30; July 17; Aug 27; Dec 13

Brokenness July 12; Oct 27; Dec 18

Comfort Feb 1; May 7, 11; June 5; July 10

Compassion Jan 12; Feb 28; Mar 7; May 5; June 4; Dec 18

Complaining Dec 2

Conflict Mar 24; May 9

Contentment Apr 9, 20; Sept 7; Nov 8, 19; Dec 10, 29

Cross Jan 6, 8, 10; Mar 1, 29; Apr 1, 2, 3, 5; May 8, 24; June 9, 12,18; July 5, 9, 27; Aug 14, 20, 31; Sept 12, 13; Oct 2, 24; Nov 12; Dec 20

Deception Sept 30; Oct 6; Dec 9, 22

Depression July 3

Despair Apr 19; July 19; Oct 11

Destiny July 15, 16, 25, 26; Aug 5; Oct 24

Discouragement Jan 19; Mar 23; Apr 29; May 6; June 3, 21; July 24, 26, 27, 31; Nov 18

Doubt May 1; June 14; July 19; Dec 16

Encouragement Jan 7; Feb 10, 19; Mar 18; Apr 22; May 2; June 15, 21; July 3, 24

Excessiveness June 7; Oct 8

Faith Feb 24; Mar 15, 26; Apr 7, 15; May 13, 20; June 14; Aug 3, 4, 19, 22; Sept 2; Nov 2, 5, 23; Dec 1, 16

Father/Child Relationship Jan 1; Apr 6, 23; June 12, 27; Sept 26; Oct 13

Fear Mar 31; Apr 30; May 1; June 25; July 19; Aug 31; Sept 2; Oct 11, 16, 27; Nov 5

Forgiveness Feb 20; Apr 1; May 31; June 30; July 17, 30; Aug 27; Sept 25; Nov 17

God's Character Jan 1, 2, 5, 7, 9, 24, 30; Feb 19, 21; Mar 12, 22, 28, 29; Apr 11, 22; May 7, 10, 27; June 4; Aug 6; Sept 23; Oct 12; Nov 15, 26; Dec 7

God's Goodness May 3; Aug 16; Oct 4, 5, 13, 21; Nov 6; Dec 23, 26

God's Nature Jan 1, 2, 7,12,18, 21, 22, 23, 24, 25, 27, 29; Feb 2, 3, 4, 5, 15, 18; Mar 4, 7, 10, 17, 18; Apr 14, 21, 23, 25; May10,11; June 10, 14, 29; July 14, 16, 22; Aug 6, 13; Sept 18, 20, 22; Oct 4, 30; Nov 2, 26; Dec 31

Grace Feb 14; Apr 1; May 5, 9, 16, 17, 18, 22; June 4, 8; Oct 22

Guard Your Heart and Mind Feb 26; Aug 8; Sept 27; Oct 6

Guidance Jan 19; May 12; June 13; Aug 2

Guilt May 25; Sept 6; Oct 3; Nov 13

Healing July 12; Aug 27

Heart Jan 20; Feb 9, 15, 28; Mar 6; May 4, 13, 15; July 22; Aug 5, 18; Oct 5, 20, 22, 26

Helplessness Sept 8

Holy Spirit Mar 9, 11; July 21; Oct 18; Nov 30

Hope Apr 19, 22, 29; June 15; July 10, 27; Aug 2; Sept 7, 13; Oct 11, 23; Dec 5, 8

Hurt Feb 20, 28; June 30; July 17, 30; Aug 9

Identity Jan 10, 12, 27; Feb 5, 7, 22; Mar 6, 8; Apr 3, 5, 14; May 8; June 12, 27, 28, 29; July 3, 13, 15, 16, 18, 25, 26; Aug 5, 10, 11, 13, 14, 20, 25; Sept 25, 26, 27; Oct 9, 13, 24; Nov 15, 18; Dec 21

Injustice Jan 16; Apr 8; July 30

Intimacy Jan 25, 26, 30; Feb 1, 2, 4, 12, 17; Mar 4, 20, 21, 27; Apr 4, 11, 16, 23, 25; June 6, 9, 10, 17, 19, 20, 22, 23; July 4; Aug 12; Sept 21; Oct 4, 5, 12, 20, 26; Nov 26

Jesus May 26, 29; June 15; July 16; Oct 23; Dec 20, 24, 25

Joy Feb 4; Mar 17, 18; June 7, 22, 26; Oct 5, 7, 21; Nov 19; Dec 26, 29

Judging Others May 28; Aug 28; Oct 18; Dec 3, 4

Lies Jan 1, 5, 6, 7, 15, 17; Feb 27; Mar 8, 23; Apr 26; May 1, 7, 10, 24; June 9, 22; July 14, 19, 24, 27; Aug 7, 13, 24, 25, 31; Sept 3, 12, 17, 25, 30; Oct 3, 23, 28, 31; Nov 13, 17, 18, 21; Dec 4, 9, 14, 21, 27

Life's Meaning Feb 6, 8; May 30; June 28; July 22; Aug 5

Life's Purpose Feb 6, 8; July 15, 20, 22, 25; Aug 5

Love Jan 10, 11, 12, 21, 22; Feb 14; Mar 4, 7, 8, 9; Apr 2,14, 23; May 3,16, 24; June 4,10, 15; Aug 12; Sept 9, 11, 15, 22; Oct 5, 14, 15, 22; Nov 14, 26; Dec 3, 25

Maturity Jan 20; Mar 3, 5, 9, 11, 13, 17, 22, 25, 27, 30; Apr 15, 17, 20, 21, 24, 26, 27; May 4, 5, 14, 15, 16, 17, 18, 20, 22; June 1, 11, 14, 17, 18, 22; July 1, 29, 30; Aug 1, 3, 29; Sept 1, 9, 10, 14, 17, 30; Oct 10, 20; Nov 2, 9, 27; Dec 31

Negative Thoughts Feb 25; Aug 24, 25

No "What-if's" Jan 7

Obedience Mar 13, 15; May 14, 20, 22

Overwhelmed Apr 28; June 3; July 11; Aug 30; Oct 16; Dec 19, 27

Patience Mar 22, 25; Apr 29; Dec 5

Peace Feb 1; Mar 24; Apr 20, 21; May 1, 18, 21; June 8, 25; July 12, 30; Aug 31; Sept 7; Oct 4, 27, 31; Nov 8, 10, 19, 29; Dec 4, 26, 27, 29

Pessimism July 8

Perfectionism Jan 15; Dec 27

Persevere Mar 19, 23; Apr 29; May 18, 21; Aug 23; Oct 19

Possibilities Mar 26; May 27; Aug 2, 28

Positive Thinking July 8; Aug 24; Sept 16; Oct 7; Nov 25; Dec 10

Potential Aug 25, 28

Power Feb 14, 20, 23; May 8; July 9, 10, 20; Aug 1; Sept 27; Nov 7, 11, 15; Dec 12

Praise Aug 26; Sept 14; Oct 26

Prayer June 2, 9; Aug 26; Dec 12, 29

Presence Jan 2; Mar 19; Apr 25, 27; May 26; July 4; Aug 10, 15; Sept 21; Oct 5, 30; Nov 14; Dec 15

Pride Apr 27; June 11; Aug 4, 18; Sept 28; Oct 1, 6, 27

Promises Jan 6, 9, 18; Mar 19; June 5, 8, 15; July 27, 31; Aug 2, 3, 17, 23; Oct 6, 24; Nov 1, 5, 16, 18, 19, 23; Dec 11

Quiet Your Mind Jan 4, 26; Apr 16; Sept 29; Oct 19; Nov 10; Dec 28

Redeemed Life Apr 5; Aug 20; Dec 6, 8

Regrets Sept 6; Nov 20

Rejection Aug 11, 13

Relationship Jan 2, 11, 17, 19, 22, 23, 27; Feb 2, 4, 5; Mar 10, 27; Apr 6, 14, 21, 23; May 7, 10; June 6, 17, 20, 27; July 4, 14, 29; Aug 1; Sept 18, 29; Oct 12, 29; Nov 4, 22, 29; Dec 1, 31

Repentance Apr 10; May 14, 28; July 1, 5; Aug 20, 30; Sept 22, 25; Nov 13; Dec 6

Rest May 7, 11; June 19; Sept 3; Nov 6

Restoration Feb 13; July 12; Nov 20

Righteousness Feb 7; Apr 7; May 25; Aug 14; Nov 17

Satan Jan 6; Mar 2; May 8; Oct 2; Nov 5; Dec 9, 11

Salvation Jan 31; Feb 7; Mar 1; Sept 4; Dec 20

Self Worth Feb 22; Aug 11

Shame Sept 6, 25; Nov 13

Sin Apr 2; Oct 3; Dec 6, 8

Sleep Mar 14; June 16; July 4

Sorrow May 14; July 1

Stress Jan 4; Apr 28; July 11; Sept 8; Dec 19, 27

Striving July 26; Nov 12

Strength Jan 24; Feb 1; Mar 18; Aug 31; Sept 19; Oct 31; Nov 7

Suffering Sept 13, 16

Surrender Jan 8; Feb 15; May 20; June 2, 7, 10, 11, 18, 26; July 17, 23, 28; Aug 4, 10, 22, 27; Sept 3, 10, 11, 22, 24; Oct 4, 10, 16, 20, 28; Nov 2, 9, 28; Dec 23

Temptation Mar 12; June 24; Oct 8; Nov 13

Thought Life Jan 5; Feb 25; Mar 13, 17, 31; Apr 10, 20; July 2, 7, 8; Aug 7, 8, 11, 13; Sept 7, 14; Oct 2, 21; Nov 20; Dec 10, 11, 13, 19

Trials Jan 14, 16, 17, 18, 20, 24; Feb 24; Mar 26, 31; Apr 9, 12, 19, 20; June 5, 18, 21; Aug 23, 30; Sept 7, 12, 19; Oct 11, 16, 31; Dec 5, 16

Trust Jan 9, 14, 16, 20, 24; Feb 20, 24; Mar 15, 16; Apr 27, 30; May 1; June 8, 14, 25; July 8, 12, 27, 31; Aug 3, 22; Sept 3, 10; Oct 6, 16, 27, 28; Nov 10, 23, 28, 29; Dec 17, 23

Truth Jan 6; Apr 26; May 9, 27; July 15; Aug 11, 13, 14, 17, 25, 30; Sept 5, 26; Oct 2; Nov 1, 16, 22; Dec 7, 9, 11

Unfairness Jan 16; Sept 12

Unforgiveness Feb 20; May 31; June 30; July 17

Unworthy May 26; Aug 11, 13; Sept 6, 25; Dec 21

Weary May 7; June 19

Work Ethic Sept 3, 24

World's Way Mar 16; Apr 8; May 15; June 1, 5, 7; July 2, 7, 22; Aug 17

Worry Mar 14; Apr 21; May 1; June 16, 25; Nov 3

Worth July 13, 18; Aug 5, 11, 13, 14

Appendix

How to Hear God's Voice
Dr. Mark Virkler

She had done it again! Instead of coming straight home from school like she was supposed to, she had gone to her friend's house. Without permission. Without our knowledge. Without doing her chores. With a ministering household that included remnants of three struggling families plus our own toddler and newborn, my wife simply couldn't handle all the work on her own. Everyone had to pull their own weight. Everyone had age-appropriate tasks they were expected to complete. At fourteen, Rachel and her younger brother were living with us while her parents tried to overcome lifestyle patterns that had resulted in the children running away to escape the dysfunction. I felt sorry for Rachel, but, honestly my wife was my greatest concern.

Now Rachel had ditched her chores to spend time with her friends. It wasn't the first time, but if I had anything to say about it, it would be the last. I intended to lay down the law when she got home and make it very clear that if she was going to live under my roof, she would obey my rules. But…she wasn't home yet. And I had recently been learning to hear God's voice more clearly. Maybe I should try to see if I could hear anything from Him about the situation. Maybe He could give me a way to get her to do what she was supposed to (i.e. what I wanted her to do). So I went to my office and reviewed what the Lord had been teaching me from Habakkuk 2:1, 2: "I will stand on my guard post and station myself on the rampart; And I will keep watch to see what He will speak to me…Then the Lord answered me and said, 'Record the vision….'"

Habakkuk said, "I will stand on my guard post…" (Hab. 2:1). The first key to hearing God's voice is to go to a quiet place and still our own thoughts and emotions. Psalm 46:10 encourages us to be still, let go, cease striving, and know that He is God. In Psalm 37:7 we are called to "be still before the Lord and wait patiently for Him." There is a deep inner knowing in our spirits that each of us can experience when we quiet our flesh and our minds. Practicing the art of biblical meditation helps silence the outer noise and distractions clamoring for our attention.

I didn't have a guard post but I did have an office, so I went there to quiet my temper and my mind. Loving God through a quiet worship song is one very effective way to become still. In 2 Kings 3, Elisha needed a word from the Lord so he said, "Bring me a minstrel," and as the minstrel played, the Lord spoke. I have found that playing a worship song on my autoharp is the quickest way for me to come to stillness. I need to choose my song carefully; boisterous songs of praise do not bring me to stillness, but rather gentle songs that express my love and worship. And it isn't enough just to sing the song into the cosmos – I come into the Lord's presence most quickly and easily when I use my godly imagination to see the truth that He is right here with me and I sing my songs to Him, personally.

"I will keep watch to see," said the prophet. To receive the pure word of God, it is very important that my heart be properly focused as I become still, because my focus is the source of the intuitive flow. If I fix my eyes upon Jesus (Heb. 12:2), the intuitive flow comes from Jesus. But if I fix my gaze upon some desire of my heart, the intuitive flow comes out of that desire. To have a pure flow I must become still and carefully fix my eyes upon Jesus. Quietly worshiping the King and receiving out of the stillness that follows quite easily accomplishes this.

So I used the second key to hearing God's voice: As you pray, fix the eyes of your heart upon Jesus, seeing in the Spirit the dreams and visions of Almighty God. Habakkuk was actually looking for vision as he prayed. He opened the eyes of his heart, and looked into the spirit world to see what God wanted to show him.

God has always spoken through dreams and visions, and He specifically said that they would come to those upon whom the Holy Spirit is poured out (Acts 2:1-4, 17).

Being a logical, rational person, observable facts that could be verified by my physical senses were the foundations of my life, including my spiritual life. I had never thought of opening the eyes of my heart and looking for vision. However, I have come to believe that this is exactly what God wants me to do. He gave me eyes in my heart to see in the spirit the vision and movement of Almighty God. There is an active spirit world all around us, full of angels, demons, the Holy Spirit, the omnipresent Father, and His omnipresent Son, Jesus. The only reasons for me not to see this reality are unbelief or lack of knowledge.

In his sermon in Acts 2:25, Peter refers to King David's statement: "I saw the Lord always in my presence; for He is at my right hand, so that I will not be shaken." The original psalm makes it clear that this was a decision of David's, not a constant supernatural visitation: "I have set (literally, I have placed) the Lord continually before me; because He is at my right hand, I will not be shaken" (Ps.16:8). Because David knew that the Lord was always with him, he determined in his spirit to see that truth with the eyes of his heart as he went through life, knowing that this would keep his faith strong.

In order to see, we must look. Daniel saw a vision in his mind and said, "I was looking...I kept looking...I kept looking" (Dan. 7:2, 9, 13). As I pray, I look for Jesus, and I watch as He speaks to me, doing and saying the things that are on His heart. Many Christians will find that if they will only look, they will see. Jesus is Emmanuel, God with us (Matt. 1:23). It is as simple as that. You can see Christ present with you because Christ is present with you. In fact, the vision may come so easily that you will be tempted to reject it, thinking that it is just you. But if you persist in recording these visions, your doubt will soon be overcome by faith as you recognize that the content of them could only be birthed in Almighty God. Jesus demonstrated the ability of living out of constant contact with God, declaring that He did nothing on

His own initiative, but only what He saw the Father doing, and heard the Father saying (Jn. 5:19, 20, 30). What an incredible way to live!

Is it possible for us to live out of divine initiative as Jesus did? Yes! We must simply fix our eyes upon Jesus. The veil has been torn, giving access into the immediate presence of God, and He calls us to draw near (Lk. 23:45; Heb. 10:19-22). "I pray that the eyes of your heart will be enlightened…." When I had quieted my heart enough that I was able to picture Jesus without the distractions of my own ideas and plans, I was able to "keep watch to see what He will speak to me." I wrote down my question: "Lord, what should I do about Rachel?"

Immediately the thought came to me, "She is insecure." Well, that certainly wasn't my thought! Her behavior looked like rebellion to me, not insecurity.

But like Habakkuk, I was coming to know the sound of God speaking to me (Hab. 2:2). Elijah described it as a still, small voice (I Kings 19:12). I had previously listened for an inner audible voice, and God does speak that way at times. However, I have found that usually, God's voice comes as spontaneous thoughts, visions, feelings, or impressions.

For example, haven't you been driving down the road and had a thought come to you to pray for a certain person? Didn't you believe it was God telling you to pray? What did God's voice sound like? Was it an audible voice, or was it a spontaneous thought that lit upon your mind?

Experience indicates that we perceive spirit-level communication as spontaneous thoughts, impressions and visions, and Scripture confirms this in many ways. For example, one definition of paga, a Hebrew word for intercession, is "a chance encounter or an accidental intersecting." When God lays people on our hearts, He does it through paga, a chance-encounter thought "accidentally" intersecting our minds. So the third key to hearing God's voice is recognizing that God's voice in your heart often sounds like a flow of spontaneous thoughts. Therefore, when I want to hear from God, I tune to chance-encounter or spontaneous thoughts.

Finally, God told Habakkuk to record the vision (Hab. 2:2). This was not an isolated command. The Scriptures record many examples of individual's prayers and God's replies, such as the Psalms, many of the prophets, and Revelation. I have found that obeying this final principle amplified my confidence in my ability to hear God's voice so that I could finally make living out of His initiatives a way of life. The fourth key, two-way journaling or the writing out of your prayers and God's answers, brings great freedom in hearing God's voice.

I have found two-way journaling to be a fabulous catalyst for clearly discerning God's inner, spontaneous flow, because as I journal I am able to write in faith for long periods of time, simply believing it is God. I know that what I believe I have received from God must be tested. However, testing involves doubt and doubt blocks divine communication, so I do not want to test while I am trying to receive. (See James 1:5-

8.) With journaling, I can receive in faith, knowing that when the flow has ended I can test and examine it carefully.

So I wrote down what I believed He had said: "She is insecure."

But the Lord wasn't done. I continued to write the spontaneous thoughts that came to me: "Love her unconditionally. She is flesh of your flesh and bone of your bone."

My mind immediately objected: She is not flesh of my flesh. She is not related to me at all – she is a foster child, just living in my home temporarily. It was definitely time to test this "word from the Lord"! There are three possible sources of thoughts in our minds: ourselves, satan and the Holy Spirit. It was obvious that the words in my journal did not come from my own mind – I certainly didn't see her as insecure or flesh of my flesh. And I sincerely doubted that satan would encourage me to love anyone unconditionally!

Okay, it was starting to look like I might have actually received counsel from the Lord. It was consistent with the names and character of God as revealed in the Scripture, and totally contrary to the names and character of the enemy. So that meant that I was hearing from the Lord, and He wanted me to see the situation in a different light. Rachel was my daughter – part of my family not by blood but by the hand of God Himself. The chaos of her birth home had created deep insecurity about her worthiness to be loved by anyone, including me and including God. Only the unconditional love of the Lord expressed through an imperfect human would reach her heart.

But there was still one more test I needed to perform before I would have absolute confidence that this was truly God's word to me: I needed confirmation from someone else whose spiritual discernment I trusted. So I went to my wife and shared what I had received. I knew if I could get her validation, especially since she was the one most wronged in the situation, then I could say, at least to myself, "Thus sayeth the Lord."

Needless to say, Patti immediately and without question confirmed that the Lord had spoken to me. My entire planned lecture was forgotten. I returned to my office anxious to hear more. As the Lord planted a new, supernatural love for Rachel within me, He showed me what to say and how to say it to not only address the current issue of household responsibility, but the deeper issues of love and acceptance and worthiness.

Rachel and her brother remained as part of our family for another two years, giving us many opportunities to demonstrate and teach about the Father's love, planting spiritual seeds in thirsty soil. We weren't perfect and we didn't solve all of her issues, but because I had learned to listen to the Lord, we were able to avoid creating more brokenness and separation.

The four simple keys that the Lord showed me from Habakkuk have been used by people of all ages, from four to a hundred and four, from every continent, culture and denomination, to break through into intimate two-way conversations with their loving Father and dearest Friend. Omitting any one of the keys will prevent you from receiving all He wants to say to you. The order of the keys is not important, just that you use them all. Embracing all four, by faith, can change your life. Simply quiet yourself down, tune to spontaneity, look for vision, and journal. He is waiting to meet you there.

You will be amazed when you journal! Doubt may hinder you at first, but throw it off, reminding yourself that it is a biblical concept, and that God is present, speaking to His children. Relax. When we cease our labors and enter His rest, God is free to flow (Heb. 4:10).

Why not try it for yourself, right now? Sit back comfortably, take out your pen and paper, and smile. Turn your attention toward the Lord in praise and worship, seeking His face. Many people have found the music and visionary prayer called "A Stroll Along the Sea of Galilee" helpful in getting them started. You can listen to it and download it free at www.CWGMinistries.org/Galilee.

After you write your question to Him, become still, fixing your gaze on Jesus. You will suddenly have a very good thought. Don't doubt it; simply write it down. Later, as you read your journaling, you, too, will be blessed to discover that you are indeed dialoguing with God. If you wonder if it is really the Lord speaking to you, share it with your spouse or a friend. Their input will encourage your faith and strengthen your commitment to spend time getting to know the Lover of your soul more intimately than you ever dreamed possible.

Is It Really God?

Five ways to be sure what you're hearing is from Him:

1. Test the Origin (1 John 4:1)

Thoughts from our own minds are progressive, with one thought leading to the next, however tangentially. Thoughts from the spirit world are spontaneous. The Hebrew word for true prophecy is naba, which literally means to bubble up, whereas false prophecy is ziyd meaning to boil up. True words from the Lord will bubble up from our innermost being; we don't need to cook them up ourselves.

2. Compare It to Biblical Principles

God will never say something to you personally which is contrary to His universal revelation as expressed in the Scriptures. If the Bible clearly states that something is a sin, no amount of journaling can make it right. Much of what you journal about will not be specifically addressed in the Bible, however, so an understanding of biblical principles is also needed.

3. Compare It to the Names and Character of God as Revealed in the Bible

Anything God says to you will be in harmony with His essential nature. Journaling will help you get to know God personally, but knowing what the Bible says about Him will help you discern what words are from Him. Make sure the tenor of your journaling lines up with the character of God as described in the names of the Father, Son and Holy Spirit.

4. Test the Fruit (Matt. 7:15-20)

What effect does what you are hearing have on your soul and your spirit? Words from the Lord will quicken your faith and increase your love, peace and joy. They will stimulate a sense of humility within you as you become more aware of Who God is and who you are. On the other hand, any words you receive which cause you to fear or doubt, which bring you into confusion or anxiety, or which stroke your ego (especially if you hear something that is "just for you alone – no one else is worthy") must be immediately rebuked and rejected as lies of the enemy.

5. Share It with Your Spiritual Counselors (Prov. 11:14)

We are members of a Body! A cord of three strands is not easily broken and God's intention has always been for us to grow together. Nothing will increase your faith in your ability to hear from God like having it confirmed by two or three other people! Share it with your spouse, your parents, your friends, your elder, your group leader, even your grown children can be your sounding board. They don't need to be perfect or super-spiritual; they just need to love you, be committed to being available to you, have a solid biblical orientation, and most importantly, they must also willingly and easily receive counsel. Avoid the authoritarian who insists that because of their standing in the church or with God, they no longer need to listen to others. Find two or three people and let them confirm that you are hearing from God! The book "4 Keys to Hearing God's Voice" is available at: www.CWGministries.org